LEXICON OF
CHEESE

Production • Origin • Types • Taste

© 2004 Rebo International b.v., Lisse, The Netherlands

Text: Anne Iburg
Typesetting: AdAm Studio, Prague, The Czech Republic
Cover design: AdAm Studio, Prague, The Czech Republic

Translation: Agentura Slůně, Ostrava for Agentura Abandon, Prague, The Czech Republic
Proofreading: Emily Sands, Jeffrey Rubinoff

ISBN 90 366 1689 1

Contents

The story of cheese

We cannot precisely say when and by whom cheese was discovered. However, one thing is clear: people discovered cheese accidentally at a time when they were settling down, ceasing their nomadic hunting and gathering lifestyle and starting to domesticate cattle.

DISCOVERING MILK

By keeping domestic animals like sheep, goats and cows, people gradually learned to use their milk. The supply of milk soon exceeded the demand, so people began storing milk in containers made of clay and wood. These containers were not easy to clean, but at that time not much attention was paid to hygiene. Due to bad cleaning, direct exposure to the sun or warmth of the fire, the milk in containers became sour and thick as it aged. Ever curious, human beings tasted these milk leftovers and found they could be eaten. Thus the first sour cream cheese came about. The natural acids in the milk, the increase in acid bacteria growth and the warmth of the fire or sunshine gave rise to sour cream cheese It quickly became a part of people's diets.

HUNTERS DISCOVER SWEET CREAM CHEESE

Sweet cream cheese was also discovered by accident. There are two legends regarding the discovery of this type of cheese. One story recounts how some hunters killed a calf during a hunt. They opened the calf's stomach and found some very tasty, white stuff. Due to the presence of an enzyme called rennet in the calf's stomach, the milk became thick.

The other legend says that the herders stored milk in dried up sheep stomachs. Due to the presence of rennet in the sheeps' stomachs, the digestive enzyme found in the digestive system of young calves, sheep and goats, the milk turned into curd in the evening. As a result of the warmth and shaking that occurred during the wandering, the herders found a liquid, whey, and white thick lumps, cheese curd.

So people learned to make cheese using the enzyme from stomachs of calves, sheep and goats. Later, people in the Mediterranean region came across two other milk thickeners: the sap from the fig tree and cleaver.

CHEESE IN ANTIQUITY

In ancient high society, people learned to make professional use of the discovery of cheese. A frieze from a temple in Mesopotamia dating back to 5000 B.C. reveals that people in the area were making sour cream cheese professionally.

The ancient Greeks also knew how to make cheese. Homer describes the magical power of cheese in his Odyssey. Goat cheese was an important commodity in Greece. It was believed that cheese made warriors stronger, that it served as an aphrodisiac and Hippocrates prescribed the use of goat cheese against inflammation. Offerings of cheese were even made to the gods.

Cheese was also highly regarded in ancient Rome. Fresh goat cheese was produced in great quantities in the center of the Roman Empire and was a staple of the Roman diet. The Romans were also familiar with the production of rennet and hard cheese. Hard cheese played an important role in the logistics and provisions of legionaries because it could be kept for a long time while the legionaries were at war in faraway corners of the Empire. The people of ancient Rome not only enjoyed the predecessors of Pecorino and Parmesan, but also tasted different kinds of cheese imported from other provinces. The prototypes of the French

Cantal and the Swiss Bergcheese were traded in Roman markets. The selection of cheese in the Roman Empire was as huge as the Empire itself and there were numerous cheese recipes. Cheese was both eaten raw and used for baking. Curing and pickling cheese in oil, wine and vinegar was especially popular since it prolonged its durability.

CHEESE IN MONASTERIES IN THE MIDDLE AGES

During the reign of Charles the Great in the early Middle Ages, the monasteries were entrusted with the task of cultivating the land and enhancing its agricultural production. Thus monks and nuns were crucial for successful cheese production and we owe the present variety of cheeses to them. Due to the writing skills of the clergy, many recipes for cheese were written down and preserved. However, it is not clear today whether the clergy invented these recipes themselves or whether they merely copied them from the local villagers. Due to the influence of monasteries, the production of cheese was optimized; cheese was one of the most important foods during the fasting period. Besides it mattered a lot to the monasteries that no one had to suffer from hunger during the winter time when milking was poor.

CHEESE TRADE DURING THE HANSEATIC PERIOD

During the Hanseatic period, cheese was commercially important. Because hard and sliced cheeses were suitable for long transports, they became important commercial goods. At the height of the Hanseatic period, the best cheese available was Dutch. The Dutch traded their cheese throughout the entire area of the Hansa, predominantly in the Baltic region. The Scandinavians, the Baltic people and the Germans tried to copy the Dutch cheese, but the outcome was less successful. During the Reformation, the Dutch started leaving their homeland for religious reasons to settle in countries such as Prussia, Denmark or Sweden where their religion was tolerated and they could enjoy the freedom they were looking for. Because they brought the know-how of quality cheese production with them, even today we can find interesting kinds of cheeses

throughout northern Europe whose production was developed and based on Gouda and Edam.

CHEESE PRODUCTION IN MODERN TIMES

In the 19th century, the last secrets regarding cheese production were disclosed. Ferdinand Cohn was the first one to discover that cheese maturation was directed by microorganisms. Pasteur, Liebig, Metchnikow and Tyndall researched rennet and the cultures that trigger spreading. In this way, the process of cheese production, as well as the biological and chemical composition of cheese, became common knowledge. Knowledge of microbiological changes combined with the technical know-how from engineers and led to a more technologically advanced cheese production and trade. Today, we can find small and large scale dairies using pasteurized milk in tanks capable of containing 2,642 gallons. They have many technical facilities at their disposal for cheese maturation. However, small-scale companies and more and more farm dairies are also on the rise. These dairies make their cheese in 26 gallon tanks where the cheese is produced and shaped manually and treated individually during the maturation period.

There is a wide range of cheese available in Europe. Apart from the cheeses protected by registered trademark, which are listed in this book, there is a wide variety of other cheeses. The production of cheese is regulated, but the recipes vary from place to place and are kept secret at every individual dairy.

The Cheese Production Process

Milk treatment at the initial stage

A milk analysis is carried out before it is further used for milk production. Purity, bacteriological composition, a high content of protein and a certain percentage of acidity are crucial for good cheese. When the milk has completed this stage of the process, it can be pasteurized. Pasteurization entails the heating of the milk at a temperature between 162° and 167°F for as long as 15 to 30 seconds. In this way, all the unwanted bacteria are killed off and the milk is sterilized. Next, the percentage of fat is established. Raw milk contains between 3.5 and 4.5% fat. Depending on the recipe, milk fat must be added or subtracted.

The thickening of the milk

The first stage of cheese production involves adding an enzyme called rennet, or sour milk bacteria, to the milk. In order for the thickening process to run smoothly, the milk kept in a tank is heated up to a temperature between 64° - 90°F and rennet or cultures of sour milk bacteria are added to the milk. The bacteria changes the sugar in the milk into acid and the protein contained in the milk curdles. This whole process can take anywhere from 10 minutes to 2 hours depending on the amount of milk and the starter cultures, and also on the temperature of the milk. During this stage, sour cream cheese is made. Sour cream cheese is not as widespread as rennet cheese. A typical sour cream cheese is turned into curds and fresh cheese or also into cheese such as Mainzer Korb-käse and other handmade cheeses.

The majority of cheeses are produced by adding rennet to the mixture. Rennet is an enzyme which is abstracted from the stomachs of calves, goats and sheep. In the past, and even today in the case of some less traditionally made cheeses, the sap from the leaves and twigs of fig trees is used. It is now possible to produce rennet genetically. The rennet is added to the heated milk which makes the protein curdle, and the milk is divided into its liquid and solid parts. Both the amount of rennet and the temperature are crucial for the consistency of the cheese. Today, a great number of sour milk bacteria are often added to rennet cheese during the production process because the milk loses these bacteria during the pasteurization. The following cheeses are made by this process: Gouda, Camembert, and Edam.

DID YOU KNOW THAT...?

A cow can give over 2,642 gallons of milk in a year? A sheep can only give between 80 to 100 gallons, a goat about 132 to 185 gallons. The amount of milk varies in all these domestic animals throughout the year. After cows, goats and sheep give birth, the milking performance is the greatest and the milk is of the highest quality. Goats and sheep, however, can only give milk half a year after giving birth. Cows are now reared to give milk at all times.

THE CHEESE CURD IS IMPORTANT FOR THE HARDNESS OF CHEESE

During the thickening process, the milk is divided into cheese curd – the firm parts of the thickening milk – and whey – the liquid part. With the help of a harp, the cheese curd is granulated to the desired level. The following rule applies during this part of the process: the finer the curd, the more whey is drained, resulting later in harder cheese.

With soft cheese, the curd is cut into pieces the size of an English walnut. With some kinds of cheese, it is not cut into slices at all. Sliced cheese is cut into the size of a pea. If the curd is so small that it is the size of a rice grain, then hard cheese is produced. For some kinds of hard cheese, the curd is heated up to a temperature between 95°F and 133°F, which results in the curd grains losing water, thus making the cheese even harder. Cheese makers call this process burning.

HOW MUCH MILK DO YOU NEED FOR 2.2 LB (1 KG) OF CHEESE?

Fresh cheese: 1 gallon
Soft cheese: 2 gallons
Sliced cheese: 3 gallons
Hard cheese: 3 – 3 ½ gallons

FORMING THE CHEESE

When the curd reaches its optimum size, it must be separated from the whey and put into a mold. Even here, various technological procedures exist. With small cheeses, the curd is separated from the whey by means of a ladle and put into another mold. The molds usually have a bottom with holes so that excess whey can be discharged.

During the production of larger cakes of cheese, the curd is lifted from the tank with a piece of cloth. First it is drained of the whey before it is put in a mold. Alternatively, the curd can be pressed out first and then either formed or sliced.

NO PRESSURE – NO HARD CHEESE

The cheese must be pressed depending on the required hardness. With soft cheese, pressing is usually not done since the weight of the cheese mass is heavy enough to discharge the whey. Also, with all sliced cheeses, the weight of the cheese itself is responsible for the desired consistency. Nevertheless, for most sliced cheeses and all hard cheeses, the curd is pressed out. The length of time, the intensity of the pressing or whether the cake of cheese will be reused, varies from cheese to cheese.

CHEESE DOES NOT TASTE GOOD WITHOUT SALT

After the cheese has taken its final shape, it will be given its taste. Salt must be added or the cheese will be bland. Depending on the kind of cheese, it is dry salted with a brush or soaked in salt brine. The time during which the cheese is soaked ranges from hours to days depending on the kind of cheese. Apart from flavoring the cheese, salt has other functions during cheese production. It takes away excess whey, helps build the crust, protects the cheese from drying up, and preserves and rectifies the maturation process.

HOW DOES CHEESE GET ITS HOLES OR "EYES?"

After a certain period of maturation, during the time when the cheese gets rid of its lactic and glutamic acids, microbes create gases such as carbon dioxide. The gas can not be released from the compact, but elastic mass and becomes trapped in the hollow places we know as "holes," or eyes.

LEAVING CHEESE TO AGE

The cheese is left to age before it goes on sale. The amount of time it is left to age depends on the kind of cheese. Soft cheese matures within a week or two. Sliced cheese needs about five weeks and hard cheese must be left to age for three months or for as long as years.

Cheese groups

In order to clearly organize the vast variety of cheeses, eight groups of cheese have been established. According to the German cheese standards, the crucial, defining feature of the cheese structure is the content of water in the fat-free cheese mass.

■ Hard cheese has the highest content of dry mass. The maximum amount of water is about 56% and the lower the amount of water the harder the cheese. However, not every type of hard cheese is as firm. Edam, for example, is a lot softer than Parmesan and can be easily cut into slices whereas Parmesan must be, in most cases, either shredded or grated. Hard cheese generally matures in about three months. However, this maturation period can last up to years, resulting in the cheese losing more water and becoming harder. German hard cheese is produced in its full fat or higher version, meaning that the cheese contains more than 45% fat in dry mass.

■ Sliced cheese has a maximum water content ranging from 54 to 63% and therefore it matures quicker and slices more easily than hard cheese. Together with Gouda, Edam and Butter-cheese, it is one of the most popular types of cheese in Germany.

■ SEMI-HARD SLICED CHEESE has a dry mass similar to that of sliced and soft cheese. Its water content lies between 61 and 69%. The majority of semi-hard sliced cheeses are produced in low – fat and double cream versions. The following kinds of cheese belong to this group: Roquefort, Tetilla and Weisslacker. The maturation period of these types varies greatly.

■ The water content in SOFT CHEESE is more than 67%. This type of cheese can have any fat content and because of its high water content, the maximum amount of fat present is lower than that of harder cheese in the same fat category.

■ PASTA FILATA is the name for a group of cheeses where the curd is scalded with hot liquid, kneaded and made into strings after it has been acidified. The origin of this cheese group can be found in Italy. It was added to the Official German List of cheese in 1999. The most well known cheeses

from this group are Mozzarella and Provolone. The water content in these cheeses ranges from 62 to 76% of dry solids.

▬ The water content of SOUR CREAM CHEESE lies between 60 and 73% of dry solids. This type of cheese is produced from low-fat sour pot cheese. That is why all these types are especially low in calories and rich in protein.

▬ PROCESSED CHEESE differs greatly from other cheese groups, because it is not produced directly from fresh milk but from a mature cheese. Scraps of different kinds of waste cheese are mixed together. The cheese mass is ground, salted and heated up. Processed cheese exists in all fat categories and in different shapes such as cubes, slices, shells, triangles, sausages and cakes.

▬ FRESH CHEESE is in its original form. After the thickening process the cheese curd is separated from the whey and it does not have to mature like so many other cheeses. The dry matter in this type of cheese makes up about 20%. That means that a double cream fresh cream cheese with 80% fat content in dry matter contains a maximum of only 16 g fat per 100 g of fresh cheese.

HOW DOES CHEESE GET ITS RIND?

The undesired rind can be found on the cheese, in a form of a whitish-greenish coat. The mold produces poisonous elements and should be discarded. In the case of hard cheese, however, the rind can be removed because other parts of the cheese are perfectly edible. The cheese has lost a lot of its water content and therefore the rind can only spread on the surface of the cheese.

Hower, one of three types of desirable rind can appear on cheese as well.

■■■ CAMEMBERT RIND: Camembert appears with a white, edible layer on the surface of the cheese. Like Brie, another soft cheese, Camembert cheese is treated with Penicillium camemberti before it matures.

■■■ ROQUEFORT RIND: The blue edible rind called *Penicillium roqueforti* is added during the production of blue rind cheese. In most cases, the cheese curd is already mixed with the rind culture. During maturation, the cheese is perforated, or pierced a few times with a needle, creating channels where oxygen can penetrate into the cheese and the rind cultures can develop. The bluish-greenish veining is found in both soft cheese and in semi-hard, sliced cheese. A combination of both rind variations is more common, as is the case with Bavaria bleu and Bresse bleu.

■■■ RED SPREAD: The surface of some cheese matures by the means of a red spread. The starter cultures used in this case are *Brevibacterium linens*, which are added to the process in the case of sour cream cheese or soft and sliced cheese. The rind of this cheese is regularly spread with the starter cultures and with salt brine during the maturation period. A red, moist, greasy rind develops.

ORGANIC CHEESE

You might have asked yourself how organic cheese differs from ordinary cheese. There is no uniform definition of organic cheese, but strict conditions have to be met so that the cheese gets a seal of approval from a recognized organic food organization. Many consumers believe that organic cheese is always made from raw milk. However, this assumption is wrong. Organic cheese is produced in much smaller amounts than ordinary cheese and it is usually hand made using traditional and rustic methods. Traditional methods of producing cheese use only natural cheese cultures and some additives like natamycine and nitrate, as well as the use of genetically engineered chymosinet (rennet), are prohibited. For example, the milk should not be purchased from farms with intensive animal rearing. The cows, sheep and goats must be kept ecologically, and fed food without any chemical additives and antibiotics. The fields and pastures belonging to the farm must be cultivated according to the regulations of a recognized, ecological farm. Synthetic fertilizers and pesticides are not allowed.

Austria at the top

Austria, a member of the European Union, devotes 10% of its total agricultural area to organic farms, and it is therefore the most important producer of organic products, especially organic cheese, in Europe. In Germany, only 1% of the total agricultural land is used for organic farming. Many organic cheeses are produced and marketed solely by the organic farmers, who also personalize the range of products to the desires of their customers.

Cheese made of raw milk

This type of milk, as its name suggests, is untreated, or heated up to a temperature no greater than 104°F so that the original bacteria are preserved. The untreated state of the milk gives this type of cheese its natural taste. However, apart from harmless germs which, no doubt, contribute nicely to the taste of the cheese, dangerous or pathogenic germs may also survive. The milk is, therefore, rigorously tested for such germs. The inspections made of producers of raw milk cheese are far stricter than those of producers making cheese from pasteurized milk. Nevertheless, only a few cases have been reported in the past 25 years in which raw milk cheese caused health problems to consumers and there is little danger in eating this type of cheese. But to be on the safe side, people with weaker immune systems, such as young children and older people should not consume unpasteurized cheese. Pregnant women are also advised not eat soft cheese made of raw milk to protect their fetus.

Consumption of hard cheese made of raw milk does not pose any health risks since the pathogenic germs are killed off during the production process, namely during the heating up of curd, the longer soaking in salt brine and the maturation period. In case of soft cheese, the danger of germs

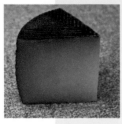

causing health problems is especially great. Soft cheese must therefore not be produced from raw milk at all.

Banning raw milk cheese: the debate

There is an increasing movement, especially within the European Union, to ban the production of cheese made from raw milk. However, many organizations, such as Slow Food, are fighting to keep it on the market. The variety of cheese production and the cheese culture would suffer a great loss if these cheeses were banned. The losses would be greater than the advantages, even in terms of health and safety issues. Many cheeses of protected origin are currently produced using raw milk. They would definitely lose something of their flavor and taste, and would probably be indistinguishable from an inferior pasteurised cheese.

YOU WILL RECEIVE MORE INFORMATION ABOUT CHEESES MADE FROM RAW MILK AT:

USA
Tel +1 718-260-8000
Fax +1 212 226 0672
info@slowfoodusa.org
20 Jay Street #313,
Brooklyn,
NYC 10013 USA

CHEESE AND ITS CONTENT

In principle, cheese is made only from concentrated milk, a fact which leads to the logical conclusion that the cheese is as healthy as its raw material. Cheese contains many of the same elements of milk: protein, fat, calcium and vitamins. Furthermore, cheese contains a large number of nutrients, which is why cheese is an important product for an optimal diet.

■■■ HOW MUCH FAT IS THERE IN CHEESE? Many people think that cheese contains a lot of fat. However, the amount of fat in cheese is greatly exaggerated and cheese has been unjustly condemned for making people fat. Regulations regarding cheese say that the fat content should not be measured in its absolute value, but as fat in dry mass. But many people are familiar with the term fat in dry mass without actually knowing what it refers to.

■■■ WHAT DOES "FAT IN DRY MASS" MEAN? The fat content of cheese can only be calculated using the dry mass of the cheese, not the weight, because during the maturation period, cheese loses water and hence changes weight. However, the dry mass does not change.

If you want to find the total fat content of a cheese, use the following rough empirical formula, which differs from type to type. Some cheeses with reduced fat content, sometimes labeled "light," indicate the fat content on the

Fresh cheese formula:
Total fat content = fat in dry mass x factor 0.3

Soft cheese such as Camembert or Brie:
Total fat content = fat in dry mass x factor 0.5

Sliced cheese such as Gouda, Tilsiter, blue rind cheese:
Total fat content = fat in dry mass x factor 0.6

Hard cheese such as Parmesan or Swiss cheese:
Total fat content = fat in dry mass x factor 0.7

packaging as an absolute value. Such a value should not be compared to the fat value in the dry mass, although it sometimes happens. Try to calculate the fat content of other cheeses using an empirical formula. You will then quickly find out that only a small saving of fat, if any, has been achieved.

■■■ THE FAT IN MILK has a high content of short-chain and mid-chain fatty acids which is why the melting point is low and the fat melts at body temperature. It also explains why milk fat is so easily digestible. The short-chain and mid-chain fatty acids influence the level of cholesterol in blood only slightly. Although cholesterol is present in cheese, you can consume it without worrying if your consumption is not excessive and the cheese is not made of full fat milk (45% fat in dry mass).

■■■ HIGH QUALITY PROTEIN: In principal, protein is composed of two basic components: 80% casein and 20% whey protein. The latter is more or less lost depending on the type of cheese after the whey has been pressed. Cheese protein contains many essential nutrients i.e. vitally important amino acids. If consumed with bread, noodles or potatoes, cheese adds great nutritional value to a meal. This means that such a meal containing amino acids meets the nutritional requirements of the human body.

■■■ CHEESE AS A SOURCE OF MINERALS AND VITAMINS: the most important mineral source in cheese is calcium, followed by magnesium. Calcium is especially important for the development and strengthening of bones and teeth. Additionally, calcium is present in numerous metabolic processes. In order to avoid osteoporosis later in life, it is absolutely necessary to eat foods with a high content of calcium. Cheese, especially sliced and hard, is a very good source of calcium.

Magnesium is also present in many metabolic processes. It activates more than 300 enzyme reactions. Magnesium is required during energy-supplying and energy-consuming reactions such as muscle contractions. It stabilizes cell membranes and at the same time, it is the psychological counter to calcium. Furthermore, it stops the development of nerve transmitters of stress hormones such as adrenalin and noradrenalin.

The more yellow the cheese, the more vitamin A and ß-carotene it contains. This vitamin is especially crucial for eyesight and for the proper function of mucous membranes. Cheese can contain a considerable amount of vitamin B. Cheese contains vitamins B2, B12 and pantothene acids which regulate and control various metabolic processes, especially for energy generation and blood development.

Enjoying cheese

People who buy cheese in bulk must have proper utensils for slicing it.

■ You need a big cheese knife with a stable blade. The cheese knife is the same size as a bread knife and has a straight, wide blade which often has a notch so that the cheese does not stick to the knife. However, this knife is only necessary if you buy large pieces of cheese or you are a cheese enthusiast, and it is not suitable for soft or sliced cheese.

■ PARMESAN CHEESE KNIFE: This knife resembles a short dagger. If you only want a few small pieces of Parmesan, you do not need this type of knife. Nevertheless, if you plan on slicing large pieces of really hard cheese, this type of knife is indispensable.

■ CHEESE SPADE: The instrument has a wide, sharp blade and a short, sturdy handle. It is used for cutting and slicing not-so-firm, hard cheeses.

■ CHEESE CHOPPER: This instrument has a relatively wide, short blade with a side handle. It is ideal for cutting and slicing normal sized pieces of cheese.

■ TWO-TOOTHED CHEESE KNIFE: The knife has a punched inner area on the blade. It is ideal for sliced cheese and soft cheese. Because there is not much of a blade, the cheese does not get stuck on the knife. The point makes eating cheese very easy.

■ CHEESE GRATER: This special tool is used by cheese enthusiasts who love eating cheese in thin slices.

■ CHEESE WIRE: This can be found in many styles. Some wires look like a saw. Some have a wire running on both sides parallel to the stick and look similar to a dagger. The metal wire is as thin as an egg slicer. This utensil should be used with rind cheeses, since the cheese is very soft and minimal cheese will get stuck on the wire.

■ CHEESE GRATERS: Each cheese grater has different sized of holes, depending on how thin the cheese slices should be. Some graters have a shape of a balk, and some are entirely flat. A luxurious version has an area into which the grated cheese falls.

■ CHEESE MILL: If you love to indulge in cheese, buy yourself a cheese mill. The cheese is cut into small pieces and then grated by hand with a crank. Sometimes you have to use a bowl for the grated cheese, but many mills are equipped with a bowl fixed under the drum.

■ GIROLLE: The Girolle cuts only one type of cheese, namely the Téte de Moine. First, remove the rind. Then, press the metal pin through the middle of the cheese to secure the grater. One can make cheese slices in a shape of a frizzy rose very easily.

MATCHING CHEESE AND WINE

Choosing the right wine to go with a particular cheese is a very tricky thing for laymen, and sometimes even for a wine connoisseur. There is absolutely no easy and general recommendation. Although there is always a wine suitable for a partiular type of cheese, these are only suggestions which can serve as a helping hand, if you need one!

In general, the following can be said about cheese and beverages, including wine, beer, cider and mineral water. All are suitable drinks to accompany cheese. However, lemonade, juice, tea and coffee are generally unsuitable, although there are exceptions from time to time. For example, some teas or grape or apple juices can accompany cheese very well. It is very common Switzerland to drink black tea with fondue and raclette.

If you are not quite sure as to what to offer your guests to drink with their cheese, or if you do not know what you should order in a restaurant, you should keep in mind the following rules.

Give preference to wine over beer
White wine over red wine
Red wine over dessert wine
Dry wine over sweet wine

▬ WHITE WINE IS VERSATILE: Many people still believe that red wine is more suitable to serve with cheese than any other wine, but heavy red wines very often have a high content of tannin, which completely drowns out the flavor, especially in smooth cheeses. Light red and white wines are ideal choices for accompanying most cheeses.

White fruity wine with lower alcohol content and acidity is a perfect match for cheese especially in the case of recently matured mild cheese. Strong, sweet white wine is also suitable for cheeses since the wine intensifies the taste of the cheese. Selecting the right wine with cheese also depends on the cheese's ripeness.

▬ CHEESE AND WINE FROM THE SAME AREA: It is not always possible (but desirable) to drink wine with cheese from the same region. The flavor of both the milk and the grapes are influenced and subject to the microclimate and the soil, which is why a wine coming from the same region as the cheese makes a perfect combination.

There are regions which produce only cheese and no wine, such as Normandy (where Camembert comes from) or Tilsiter near the Baltic Sea. In this case, the rule does not need to be so strictly observed. Anyhow, it is a pity to drink Barolo with Mozzarella merely because both products come from Italy.

How to Choose the Correct Wine for Cheese

▬ Curd cheese:
White wine: half dry, seasoned Silvane, Rivane, dry, light wines as e.g. Green Valtelline, Riesling, white Sauvignon as well as Champagne, sparkling wines or Prosecco.
Rosé wine: Portugal

▬ Young goat cheese:
White wine: Young Sauvignon, fiery Riesling or Sancerre
Rosé wine: Côtes de Provence
Red wine: Young Beaujolais, Chinon, Dornfeld or blue Frankish wine

▬ Mellow goat cheese:
White wine: at least 3 years matured Sauvignon or Chardonnay
Red wine: heavy red wines from Côtes du Rhône or from Languedoc-Roussillon

▬ Soft cheese with white rind:
White wine: White or gray burgundy or Chardonnay
Red wine: Late Burgunde, Portugal, Lemberger or Shiraz

■ CHEESE WITH BLUE RIND:
White wine: Wine from withered grapes, Traminer, Scheurebe or Sauternes; Sherry and Portwein
Red wine: Pomerol or burgundy

■ CHEESE WITH RED SPREAD:
White wine: Spicy Traminer or Muscat d'Alsace
Red wine: Languedoc, Cahors, Pomerol or Corvo

■ FINE SLICED CHEESE:
White wine: seasoned Riesling, Weißburgunder
Red wine: mild late burgundy or Beaujolais

■ SPICY HARD CHEESE:
White wine: Fendant
Rosé wine: Tavel
Red wine: Merlot, Cabernet Sauvignon or Barolo

■ SOUR MILK CHEESE:
Beer or cider or no wine

How to Arrange a Cheese Plate

A cheese plate can be arranged using only three or four different kinds of cheese. The choice depends on the occasion, the time of day, the season, and the menu – as well as on the number of guests. It is best to choose at least one representative from each of the great cheese families so that there is something to suit all tastes.

■ THE RIGHT AMOUNT! In planning a cheese plate, choosing the correct amount of cheese is as important as choosing the right type. When the cheese is a main dish, at an evening cheese and wine party, for example, ½ lb per person is perfect. 2 to 3 oz per person will be sufficient when the cheese is part of a dessert or offered at a brunch.

The correct arrangement of the cheese plate is difficult: Cheese should not be randomly piled on a plate. The cheeses should be arranged clockwise according to the content of their spices, or their aroma and taste. It is possible to ask for advice in the cheese shop or to observe the following fixed rules: mild curd cheese, than young soft cheese followed by young goat cheeses, then sliced and hard cheeses, then matured goat cheeses and soft cheeses with white rind and intense flavor. The end of the row should be made up of piquant cheeses with red or blue cultures. A simpler formula is to place the most delicate cheese at the top right, followed by the spicy kinds. The circle should end with sharp-tasting cheeses. A wooden board, marble board or common dessert plate are the best options.

▰ IDEAS FOR CHEESE PLATES:

Italian cheese plate: Provolone, Fontina, Taleggio, Gorgonzola

French cheese plate: Picodon, Brie de Melun, Morbier, Beaufort, Munster, Roquefort

Cheese plate "Normandie": Neufchatel, Camembert, Pont-l'Evéque, Livarot

Cheese plate "Jura": Comté, Bleu de Gex, Vacherin du Haut-Doubs

Cheese plate "Midi": Cabécou, Ossau-Iraty, Roquefort

Cheese plate "Auvergne": Cantal, Saint-Nectaire, Fourme d'Ambert, Laguiole

Spanish cheese plate: Tetilla, Ibores, Idiazábal, Cabrales

Cheese plate for brunch: processed double cream curd cheese from Brie, Gouda, Emmenthal, Bavaria blu

Cheese plate for serving in open areas: Altenburg goat cheese, Jarlsberg, Tilsiter, Havarti, Stilton

Cheese plate for beer: Cheddar, middle-aged Gouda, processed Harzer, Limburger

Mediterranean cheese plate: Mozzarella, Brocciu, Manchego, Roquefort

Cheese plate "International Highlights": Camembert de Normandie, Manchego, Greyerzer, Taleggio, Roquefort

▰ WITH OR WITHOUT THE RIND

There are no fixed rules. Follow your instinct! The rinds, naturally, must be cut off hard cheeses. In the case of cheeses with red culture or white rinds, it is a question of taste. These cheeses are more aromatic with the rind because it has the sharpest taste. People

NOTE!

The cheese must have the opportunity to develop its aroma. For this reason, you need to take the cheese out half an hour before the beginning of the meal.

who like milder taste should cut off the rind. But if you enjoy really pungent cheese, consume these cheese in their entirety.

WHICH BREAD IS BEST SUITED FOR A CHEESE?

When we have elected the right cheese for the cheese plate, a new question arises, namely which type of bread is suitable?

Before making a decision, remember that you cannot spoil anything by the choice of bread. The person who wants to serve an exotic, and therefore risky, new bread will be glad to know that a great variety of bread sits well with cheese. But if we know what our guests prefer, then they should be offered their favorite bread and the decision is a simple one.

Serve the cheese as a whole piece, unpacked. Do not cut it into slices. The matured cheeses could melt or turn dry, spoiling the appearance of the plate and the flavor. Accompany with suitable knives.

CULINARY PAIRING: BREAD AND CHEESE:

▬ MILD SLICED CHEESE: Whole-meal bread, Baguette, rye bread

▬ NUTTY SLICED CHEESE: ham bread, mixed wheat bread

▬ SOFT, INTENSELY FLAVORED CHEESE WITH RED RIND: mixed wheat bread, bread roll, wholemeal bread, caraway bread

---

UNUSUAL COMBINATION: PIQUANT AND SWEET.

Some people refuse cheese with jam while others consider it a delicacy. If you belong to the latter group and enjoy combining piquant with sweet, try combining raisins and cheese with red rind in a sandwich. Some very zesty cheeses include Munster or blue cheese Bleu d'Auvergne.

■ SLICED CHEESE OR SOFT CHEESE WITH SLIGHT RIND: ham bread, Graham bread, crispbread

■ STRONG SOFT CHEESES WITH WHITE RIND: mixed wheat bread, bread roll

■ MILD SOFT CHEESE WITH WHITE RIND: pumpernickel, sunflower seed bread, darker rye bread and Graham bread

■ FULL-FAT BUTTER SLICED CHEESE: bread roll, mixed wheat bread, nutty crispbread

■ NUTTY, SPICY HARD CHEESE: rye bread, Graham bread

■ SHEEP'S MILK CHEESE: ham bread, rye bread, olive bread, crispbread

■ GOAT'S MILK CHEESE: ham bread, rye bread, rye whole meal bread

■ CHEESE WITH BLUE RIND: sesame bread, pumpernickel, rye, wholemeal bread

HOW TO SERVE CHEESE

Serve cheese in pieces, uncovered. Do not chop. Mature cheese can be soft. You should not serve chopped slices, because they get stale or moldy quickly and will look unappetizing on your Cheese plates - not to mention the terrible taste! Appropriate knives must be used.

AND WHAT ELSE GOES WITH CHEESE?

Cheese with bread and wine makes an almost perfect meal, but it can be improved with fruits and vegetables. To harmonize the whole meal, try the following list of combinations:

- **CRUDE CHEESE**: strawberry, mango, orange, tomatoes, radish, herbs, rucola and celery
- **SOFT CHEESE WITH WHITE RIND**: grapes, figs, walnuts, tomatoes, radishes, herbs and paprika
- **SOFT CHEESE WITH RED SPREAD**: raisins, dried figs, onion and spring onion
- **CHEESE WITH BLUE RIND**: pears, apples, dates, walnuts, and celery and fennel bulb
- **SLICED CHEESE**: grapes, mandarin oranges, tomatoes, paprika, pickles and radishes
- **HARD CHEESE**: grapes, walnuts, tomatoes, pickles, radishes and salad
- **GOAT'S MILK CHEESE**: figs, pears, tomatoes, rucola, olives and paprika
- **SHEEP'S MILK CHEESE**: grapes, figs, tomatoes, olives and paprika

HINTS TO LEXICON ON CHEESE

The following hints are here to help you orient yourself when using this Lexicon.

The names of the cheeses are arranged in alphabetical order and grouped with similar types. It is helpful to look in the index when you cannot find your cheese.

The box on the margin indicates the most important characteristics at a glance, including the pronunciation of the name, the type of milk and the origin. Accompanying drink suggestions are also given. The symbols have the following meanings:

Cow's milk: 🐄
Sheep's milk: 🐑
Goat's milk: 🐐
Crude milk: ⬜
Pasteurized milk: ⬜

Please note that the fat content given is the most common fat content. As a rule, it is the minimum fat content permissible.

Abondance

Milk:
🐄 🥛

Country of origin:
France

Recommended drink:
White wine, e. g. Fendant

▬ TYPE: Hard cheese

▬ ORIGIN AND EXTENT: This French mountain cheese was invented in a monastery called Abondance in the 5th century. A monastery of the same name is located in Haute-Savoie, French Alps.

▬ FEATURES: The round cheese weighs from 15 to 27 lb. Its diameter is between 15 to 17 in. Its height is 3 in and its margin is slightly concave. The rind is, depending on age, orange-yellow colored and smooth, or brown and corrugated. Its consistency is velvety and contains small holes.

▬ PRODUCTION: Abondance is a raw milk cheese and it is obtained from the milk of cows in Abondance. This race is accustomed to rough mountain climates. The dark colored cheese, produced from summer milk, has a very aromatic flavor. Immediately after milking, the still-warm milk is processed by adding rennet. Thickened milk is heated while stirring until the curds are firm with holes. The cheese is then packed into cloth and molded with a wooden circle and then pressed. It is matured for a minimum of 90 days.

IN THE KITCHEN

AROMA:
Abondance has a fruity nut flavor.

FAT CONTENT:
48% fat in dry mass.

USE:
Potato cake with Abondance is a regional specialty, which you can enjoy in the agreeable atmosphere of mountain villages in Abondance. These villages belong to the well-known ski region Portes du Soleil.

DO YOU KNOW THAT?

This cheese became famous when the abbey Abondance was chosen as the official supplier for the election of the Pope in the year 1381. The monastery delivered 1.5 tons of Abondance cheese to Avignon.

PURCHASE/STORAGE:
Abondance can be bought only in specialized cheese shops. The cheese from milk is protected by AOC (Appelations d'Origine). It is recommended to choose summer-Abondance and to always buy a whole piece. The cheese is best stored with cheeses of the same type in grease-proof paper in a plastic box in a refrigerator at home at 50° F.

Mountain Cheese from Allgau

Milk:
🐄 ▯

Country of origin:
Germany

Recommended
drink:
White wine,
E.g. gray burgundy

■ TYPE: Hard cheese

■ ORIGIN AND EXTENT: Mountain Cheese from Allgau is a type of cheese which is protected and may be produced only in Lindau, Upper, East and Lower Allgau, Ravensburg and Bodensee as well as in the towns of Kempten, Kaufbeuren and Memmingen.

■ FEATURES: Mountain Cheese from Allgau has a smaller body than Emmenthal from the same region. Its weight is from 27 to 110 lbs. The holes are also smaller and the curds are darker.

■ PRODUCTION: Mountain Cheese from Allgau is produced similarly to Emmenthal, but in small production places – in chalets in the Allgau Alps and in cheese plants, mostly in Upper Allgau at a height between 900 to 1800 m. It is produced only from raw milk and it reaches maturity in a minimum of 4 months. Some sorts, however, must mature for up to one year and after this time their spicy aroma will be fully developed.

IN THE KITCHEN

AROMA:
The more mature Mountain Cheese from Allgau has a more intensive and spicy flavor.

FAT CONTENT:
50% fat in dry mass

USE:
This cheese is suitable for brunch during trips to the mountains. It can be cut into small cubes for various salads and its melting qualities make it well suited for baking puddings and toasts.

PURCHASE/STORAGE:
Mountain Cheese from Allgau can be bought without problems in any milk shop in southern Germany. Elsewhere, you must find special cheese shops. Mountain Cheese is also offered in supermarkets, but this cheese is probably not produced from raw milk in small chalets. Packing up the cheese and keeping it in the refrigerator is the best way to store this cheese.

Goat Cheese from Altenburg

Milk:

Country of origin:
Germany

Recommended
drink:
White wine e.g.
Silvaner

■ TYPE: Soft cheese

■ ORIGIN AND EXTENT:
Goat Cheese from Altenburg comes from the boundary between Thuringia and Saxony. It may only be produced in the regions of Altenburg, Schmölln, Gera, Zeitz, Geithain, Grimma, Wurzen, Borna and in the town Gera.

■ FEATURES: The round-shaped loaf of cheese is 4 in in diameter and has a height of 1 in. Its weight is 9 oz. The surface is covered with a white Camembert mold. The curd is pale yellow, plastic and full of holes. The small brown spots in the curd are caraway seeds.

■ PRODUCTION: Goat Cheese from Altenburg is produced from cow's milk with the addition of 15% of goat's milk. The milk is processed by adding rennet and then it is cut into rough pieces. Before the formation of the cheese, caraway seeds are added. The cheese matures within a period of ten days.

IN THE KITCHEN:

AROMA:
Goat Cheese from Altenburg has an intense flavor with a potent caraway taste.

FAT CONTENT:
30% fat in dry mass.

USE:
Goat Cheese from Altenburg is traditionally consumed with bread. With some pickles or beets it creates a good brunch.

PURCHASE/STORAGE:
Goat Cheese from Altenburg can be bought in any larger cheese shop in Thuringia and Saxony. In other parts of Germany, it can be bought only in speciality cheese shops. The cheese can be storied for a short period of time in the refrigerator, tightly packed.

Appenzell Cheese

Milk:
🐄 🥛

Country of origin:
Switzerland

Recommended
drink:
Red wine,
e.g. late burgundy

TYPE: Slicing cheese

ORIGIN AND EXTENT: This cheese comes from Swiss cantons Appenzell, Inner and Außerrhoden. Today, this cheese is produced also in parts of cantons St. Gallen and Thurgau.

FEATURES: The weight of the round-shaped cheese is about 15 lb. Its diameter is 12 to 13 in and has a height 3 to 3½ in. The natural crust is red to dark brown and scarred. The dough is finely perforated and has a plastic consistency. The holes' diameter is ¹⁄₁₀ to ½ in and they are regularly extended.

PRODUCTION: The milk comes from hay-fed cows. 4,227 gallons are processed per day. During the first stage, the milk is cooled to 50°F and centrifuged to adjust the exact fat content. Then the milk is heated in vessels with a maximum volume of 1,585 gallons while stirring at a temperature of 88°F. Rennet and lactic acid are added. After about 30 to 40 minutes, the milk is curdled and the clots cut into pieces. When the curd reaches the magnitude of corn grains, the whey is drained. The curd is then heated again and the cheese mass attains the necessary solidity. Next, the cheese is formed, pressed and stored in shelves for draining together with the mold. The cheese is then put into brine, which is important for the formation of the

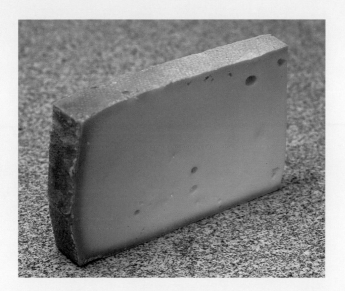

crust and for the flavor and durability of the cheese. Appenzell cheese matures at around 57° to 59°F with 90% relative humidity for a minimum of 3 months. After this time, the cheese is cured with herb brine, a secret composition of cheese producers.

▬ HISTORY: Formerly Appenzell cheese was one of the many traditional Alpine cheeses, also known as "tax cheeses" because they were used by farmers to pay taxes.

Swiss Bread Soufflé

■ INGREDIENTS: 1 large onion • 1 cup mushrooms • 2 tablespoons oil • 1 lb turkey steaks • 1 teaspoon rose paprika • 1 cup cream • 2 cups vegetable stock • 1 teaspoon starch • salt and pepper to taste • ½ baguette • 5 oz Appenzell cheese • 1 cup milk • 2 eggs

■ PREPARATION: Cut the onion into small pieces. Pare the cloves of garlic and press, clean the mushrooms and cut into fine slices.

Cut the meat into small pieces, roast in oil until they turn brown and remove from heat. Roast the onions and garlic until glassy, add the mushrooms, dust with paprika and heat briefly. Add cream and stock. Now allow it to cook 5 minutes until it bubbles gently. Mix the starch with a small amount of water and add to the sauce. Add the meat and the spices. Cut baguette into chunks. Mix the milk and eggs and add the spices. Pour the meat mixture over the bread and sprinkle with the cheese. Flood with the egg mixture. Bake at 392°F for about 30 minutes.

In the kitchen

Aroma:
Appenzell cheese has a fully spicy and fine flavor.

Fat content:
48% Fat in dry mass.

Use:
Thanks to its excellent melting qualities, Appenzell cheese is the perfect cheese for soufflés, as an ingredient in sauces and for preparation of cheese fondue. In Appenzell, it is customary to also add several slices of cheese to baked potatoes or to fried eggs.

Purchase/storage:
Appenzell cheese can be found in any large cheese shop.
Store at home in the refrigerator, alone or with other cheeses of the same type, packed in grease-proof paper and perforated foil.

Asiago d'allevo

Pronunciation:
Asjago dallewo

Milk:

Country of origin:
Italy

Recommended drink:
Red wine, e.g.
Marzemino from
Trentino

■ TYPE: Slicing cheese

■ ORIGIN AND EXTENT: Asiago originates in the provinces Vicenza and Trient, as well as in some provincial villages in Padua and Treviso.

■ FEATURES: Asiago d'allevo is round, cylindrical cheese, with a height of 3½ to 5 in, a diameter of 12 to 14 in and an almost straight margin. It weighs between 18 to 27 lb and has a smooth and uniform rind. Asiago of intermediate age has light yellow, compact curd with small and intermediate holes. Older Asiago has a grainier consistency than "intermediately old" cheese.

■ PRODUCTION: The milk, diluted by rennet, is separated from the cream. After storing the raw cheese for thickening, the whey is left to drain and the cheese mass is put into special forms called "fascere." Salt is added to the dry cheese or to the lightly brined cheese. Asiago cheese is known as "intermediately old" or "old" according to the maturation period, which may last for up two years.

Asiago pressato is similarly prepared from whole milk and has a minimum dry substance fat content of 44%. It does not differ

much in appearance from the original cheese. Unlike Asiago d'allevo, this cheese is pressed and the maturing period is only 20 to 40 days. We can find it mostly in cheese shops and its flavor is much finer.

Asparagus risotto

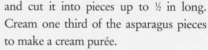

■ INGREDIENTS: 6 stems green asparagus • 6 stems white asparagus • salt • 1 teaspoon butter • 1 pinch sugar • 2 tablespoons cream • 1 onion • 2 teaspoons oil • 1 cup risotto-rice • ½ cup dry white wine • pepper • 3½ oz Asiago

■ PREPARATION: Wash the green asparagus, pare the white asparagus and cut off the woody ends. Cook the white asparagus for 12 to 15 minutes and the green asparagus for 10 minutes in salted water with butter and a pinch of sugar. When the asparagus can be bitten through, take it out from the water and let the water drain. Cut off the tips of the asparagus and cut it into pieces up to ½ in long. Cream one third of the asparagus pieces to make a cream purée.

Pare and mince the onion, then put into oil and stew it gently. Add the rice and cook until golden.

Mix 3 cups asparagus stock with white wine, add this mixture slowly to the rice and stir until the whole liquid is spent. Add salt and pepper to the finished risotto, then the asparagus purée, the pieces of asparagus and the cheese and mix the whole mixture thoroughly.

IN THE KITCHEN

AROMA:
Asiago is mildly spicy with a nutty and slightly lemony flavor.

FAT CONTENT:
34% fat in dry mass.

USE:
Middle-aged Asiago suits ciabatta well. Old Asiago can be grated over polenta, pasta, soups and risotto.

PURCHASE/STORAGE:
Asiago can be bought in cheese shops or Italian specialty shops. It can be stored in a vegetable box in the refrigerator.

HAVE YOU TRIED...?

POLENTA-SOUFFLÉ: **Arrange the polenta slices, ground meat and grated Asiago into soufflé form. Add small pieces of butter between layers. Bake at 356°F for about 30 minutes. If somebody prefers not to eat meat, then you may use tomatoes stewed with onions instead of meat. The last layer: tomato purée, flakes of butter and Asiago.**

Azeitão

Milk:
🐑 🍶

Country of origin:
Portugal

Recommended
drink:
Red wine
e.g. Quinta de
camarata

■ TYPE: Slicing cheese

■ ORIGIN AND EXTENT: The home of this cheese is Setúbal, south of Lisbon. It is named for the village Azeitão.

■ FEATURES: Azeitão is a small, round cheese with a diameter of ½ to 1 in and a height 1½ to 2 in. Its weight varies between 3½ to 9 oz. Its curd is a white to pale yellow color sometimes with a small number of holes. Its natural rind is a reddish orange color.

■ PRODUCTION: Azeitão is produced from raw sheep's milk. After thickening, the whey is left to drain slowly. After salt is added, the cheese is stored for twenty days at a temperature of 50° to 54°F and at a relative humidity of 85% to 90%.

In the kitchen

Aroma:
Azeitão has the delicate flavor of sheep's milk and is slightly acidic.

Fat content:
45% fat in dry mass.

Use:
Azeitão is suitable with a glass of wine or as a part of a cheese plate.

Purchase/storage:
Azeitão can be bought in a cheese shop or in a Portuguese specialty shop. It can be stored in the vegetable box of a refrigerator.

Beaufort

Milk:
🐄 🥛

Country of origin:
France

Recommended
drink:
Rosé or White
wine, e.g.
Chardonnay

▬ TYPE: Hard cheese

▬ ORIGIN AND EXTENT: Beaufort is a mountain cheese. Its name is the name of a small village near Albertville, where the cheese was originally prepared. Nowadays, the cheese is from Savoy, in the French Alps, and is protected.

▬ FEATURES: The cheese is shaped like a water wheel. With a diameter of 24 in and a height of 8 in, it is not small. Its margin is slightly rounded and its weight varies between 88 to 132 lb. Its rind is natural, dark yellow colored and very thin.

▬ PRODUCTION: The milk for Beaufort cheese is taken from the cows of Tarentaise and comes exclusively from the High Alps. In summer, the cows pasture on high-mountain pastures above the tree level and the cheese is produced in chalets. 132 gallons of milk are consumed for one cheese and one cow gives 793 gallons milk annually. Therefore, it is possible to produce 6 cheeses from one cow per year.

For the production of Beaufort, warm milk is curdled by adding rennet. The curdled milk is cut with a wire knife. The mixture of curds and whey is heated while stirring over an open fire. The cheese is subsequently packed into cloth and the whey is left to drain. Then the cheese is molded into a circle of beech wood and pressed.

Semi-finished cheese is matured for 6 months in cold cellars. Beaufort cheeses, after maturing for more than 6 months, may be named "high-mountains."

▬ HISTORICAL NOTE: Beaufort cheese represented the only opportunity for poor farmers to make a profit. Cheese with long-term durability was sold in large towns and the farmers consumed it themselves only on extraordinary occasions.

Savoyard vegetable soup

■ INGREDIENTS: 3½ oz streaky bacon • 2 onions • 3 pieces leek • 4 carrots • 1 celery • 3 potatoes • 1 quart water • 3½ tablespoons milk • 2 tablespoonfuls créme fraiche • 4–8 sage leaves • salt• 8 slices of rye bread • 3 tablespoons butter • 5 oz Beaufort

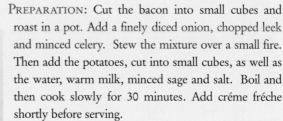

■ PREPARATION: Cut the bacon into small cubes and roast in a pot. Add a finely diced onion, chopped leek and minced celery. Stew the mixture over a small fire. Then add the potatoes, cut into small cubes, as well as the water, warm milk, minced sage and salt. Boil and then cook slowly for 30 minutes. Add créme fréche shortly before serving.
Butter the slices of bread, spread with grated Beaufort and put two slices into each soup plate. Flood with hot soup and serve immediately.

IN THE KITCHEN

AROMA:
Beaufort has a fresh smell and a mildly salty flavor.

FAT CONTENT:
48% fat in dry mass.

USE:
Beaufort's excellent melting qualities allow it to be used in the preparation of soufflé, baked potatoes and rösti as well as in quiches und omelets.

PURCHASE/STORAGE:
Beaufort is popular in Germany and is traditionally enjoyed during ski trips in the French Alps. It can be found in numerous special cheese shops and should be bought in individual pieces. At home, it should be stored at 50°F in the refrigerator. It is best to store this cheese alone, packed in grease-proof paper in a plastic box.

HAVE YOU TRIED...?
Serve Beaufort with gourd bread and cold rosé, e.g. Côtes de Provence.

Bleu d'Auvergne

Milk:
🐄 🥛

Country of origin:
France

Recommended drink:
Côtes du Rhône,
Cahors, but also
sweet wines,
such as Sauternes

■ TYPE: Semi-hard, sliced cheese with internal mold

■ ORIGIN AND EXTENT: This French cheese with its blue mold was originally regarded only as an imitation of the famous Roquefort. Today, it is one of best known cheeses in Auvergne, in the regions Cantal and Puy-de-Dôme. In 1975, it obtained the AOC impression, which states the area of origin and production.

■ FEATURES: The cheese is molded in flat cylindrical forms of different diameters. The large loaves of Bleu d'Auvergne have a diameter of 8 in and a height of 4 in and its weight is 3 to 7 lb. Small loaves have a diameter of only 4 in and a weight of 12 oz, 1 lb or 2.2 lb. They are packed in aluminum foil. The cheese has thin blue veins and only a thin external rind.

■ PRODUCTION: The cheese is prepared by adding rennet. After slicing and mixing the spores of blue mold, the cheese is put into molds and the whey is left to drain. The cheese is equipped with air channels so that the noble mold can be created. It is matured in ventilated cellars where large cheeses finish after 4 weeks. Smaller after 3 weeks.

■ HISTORICAL NOTICE: A legend says that a farmer's son named Antoine Roussel once got the idea to add blue mold,

which he found on rye bread, to the sour milk. Then he perforated the cheese with a needle. Thus numerous mold veins were formed and the cheese got its special aroma.

■■■ OTHER BLUE CHEESE WITH THE AOC IMPRESSION: *Bleu des Causses.* In the high limestone mountain plains of Central massif, we can find small cheese workshops, a long-standing characteristic of the region. A rocky pasture with a rough climate rich in contrasts gives Bleu des Causes its spices. The cheese matures over a period of 3 to 6 months in the natural caves of limestone rocks. Humid and cold air streams blow through the caves and give the cheese its characteristic nutty flavor.

Bleu du Haut-Jura or Bleu de Gex. Only the milk of Montbéliard cows, which pasture on fruity pastures of Jura, is used in its production. The cheese is prepared from raw milk and has a more expressive flavor than other Bleus. The lower side of cheese, is stamped with the verb "Gex." It has a mild flavor, somewhat like a hazelnut.

Bleu du Vercors-Sassenage. The traditional mountain cheese from the Rhone Alps was first prepared by monks. The recipe soon spread into the surrounding villages. Since 1998, this cow's milk cheese from the region of the French Alps bears the AOC–impression. It has a mild flavor and slight hazelnut aroma.

Bleu de Bresse comes from Bresse in Burgundy. It is a hybrid of blue cheese and soft cheese with a white rind. It is produced industrially in large amounts from pasteurized cow's milk and is, therefore, stronger than other Bleu cheeses with an AOC–impression.

In the kitchen

Aroma:
The creamy cheese Bleu d'Auvergne has a strong, salty flavor.

Fat content:
50% fat in dry mass.

Use:
This cheese is traditionally served with grapes after meals. Bleu d'Auvergne mixed with butter is served with an aperitif. Bleu d'Auvergne is also well suited for creative cooking. The cheese is used as a flavoring for salads and soufflé. Quiche containing this cheese has an especially strong aroma. Bleu de Gex is very good when spread on a slice of rye bread.

Purchase/storage:
Bleu d'Auvergne can be found in French specialty shops or in delicatessens offering large cheeses. It is not recommended for long-term storage at home. When packed separately, it can be stored in a refrigerator at 50°F and it should be removed from the refrigerator 1 hour before meals so that its aroma can be fully savored.

> ## Have you tried...?
> **Bleu d'Auvergne with warm hazelnut bread – excellent!**

Brie

Milk:
🐄 🥛

Country of origin:
France

Recommended drink:
Red wine
e.g. Bordeaux or
Côtes du Rhône

■ TYPE: Soft cheese

■ ORIGIN AND EXTENT: Brie comes from Ile de France. The name comes from the name of the region east of Paris. Before the railway system was developed, it was not possible to transport this cheese long distances without spoiling it. Thus, only Parisians could enjoy this cheese and it became known as "Parisian cheese." In France, there are two kinds of Brie cheese, bearing the AOC- impression: Brie de Meaux and Brie de Melun.

■ FEATURES: In France, Brie cheese follows strict guidelines. It is a soft cheese with an external mold layer with minimum fat content of 40% fat in its dry substance and 44% dry substance in the whole mass. The cheese has the shape of a flat cake with a diameter 10 to 16 in. Cheeses with diameters of 6 to 9 in are allowed to be sold.

■ PRODUCTION: Brie matures from the inside out and within several days, a cover of mold encloses the whole cheese. Industrially produced cheese differs from that produced in home workshops mainly in the following respect: it is always produced from pasteurized milk and can be stored for a long time in cooled shelves in of supermarkets.

■ BRIE WITH AOC-IMPRESSION: *de Meaux* was offered as a dessert to the deputies of the Wiener Congress in the years 1814-1815. Since then, Brie has been imitated throughout Europe. Unlike "normal" Brie, the origin of which is not protected, the AOC-cheese Brie de Meaux may only come from the area of Ile-de-France near Paris. According to tradition, it may be produced only from crude milk. By means of a "Brie shovel," the curd is separated from the whey and is poured manually into molds. After drying, it is salted and then the cheese slowly and uniformly matures for a time period of no less than 4 weeks. During this time, it is turned over several times manually.

Brie de Meaux Because of its smaller diameter, the Brie de Meaux is seen as the "younger" brother of Brie de Meaux. This raw milk cheese has a much stronger aroma as well as a saltier taste, depending on the production method used. Thanks to rennet treatment, the Brie de Meaux turns sour in less than 30 minutes, whereas Brie de Meaux, with the use of lactic acid bacteria, needs a minimum of 18 hours. Then the cheese is formed either by hand or with a ladle. It reaches its maturity in a period of no less than 4 weeks.

■ OTHER TYPES OF BRIE CHEESE: *Coulommiers* comes from the town of the same

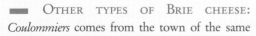

name in Ile de France and it matures within 2 weeks. Since it is produced industrially, it is readily available and can be found everywhere. It belongs to the Brie family, but it is one third the size of the largest Brie. Its flavor is delicate and delightful.

Fougeru differs from the other family members because on its surface is a fern leaf. It is similar to Coulommiers in flavor and mode of production.

German Brie is a copy of the French originals. It is produced in sizes ranging from 2.2 to 7 lb and matures according to the size over a maximum period of 4 weeks. During the maturation process, the consistency does not change much. This Brie is also available with herbs and spices, which are added to the cheese curd before it matures.

▬ GOAT BRIE: We can also find numerous regional Brie cheeses connected with the production of biological products. They are lighter colored than their relatives produced from cow's milk and have a more expressive flavor.

In the kitchen

Aroma:
The flavor of Brie ranges from finely acidic to potent, according to age and type. Brie cheese from raw milk is more aromatic.

Fat content:
30 to 60% fat in dry mass.

Use:
Because of their higher fat content, Brie cheeses are suitable for the preparation of soufflé, baked potatoes or roasted potatoes and melted in sauces of the Béchamel type. The internal part of cheese is usually mixed with spices and herbs and is used for spreading on bread. Brie is best when it is yellow gold and soft, but does not spread.

Purchase/storage:
Unusual kinds, such as Brie de Melun and Brie de Meaux, can only be found in specialized cheese shops. Goat's milk Brie can be found in eco-shops. Industrially produced Brie can be stored in the refrigerator at 50°F. Manually produced Brie should be consumed on the day of purchase or 1 to 2 days after. Brie is best stored alone, packed with grease-proof paper and inside a plastic box.

Brocciu

Milk:

Country of origin:
France

Recommended
drink:
White Sauvignon
or Côtes du
Rhône

TYPE: Soft cheese

ORIGIN AND EXTENT: The home of Brocciu is Corsica. It is the only cheese with an AOC-impression that comes from Corsica and must be produced in departments in Corse-du-Sud and Haute-Corse.

FEATURES: The Brocciu cheese is typically cone-shaped and is permitted to be produced in 4 sizes: about ½ lb, 1 lb, 2.2 lb and 7 lb. It is known as fresh raw cheese under the name "Brocciu frais" and matures as "Brocciu sec" or "Brocciu passu."

PRODUCTION: Goat and sheep whey is mixed with goat and sheep's milk during the production of the cheese. The whey is a waste product from the production of soft or sliced cheeses and must come from regional milk workshops. The whey is heated to 104°F and salt and raw milk are subsequently added. The amount of milk must be no greater than 35% of the amount of whey. It is then mixed and heated from 176° to 194°F, before the foam is removed and the mixture is poured into a container to drain. It is sold as a soft curd cheese in various stages of its maturity. The finished cheese must mature for a minimum of 15 days in the region of its origin, and be salty on the surface.

IN THE KITCHEN

AROMA:
As curd cheese, Brocciu has a fresh, fine flavor. The matured is more expressive, salty and acrid.

FAT CONTENT:
40% fat in dry mass.

USE:
In Corsica, Brocciu is a staple of many regional dishes and is used for baking breads.

DO YOU KNOW THAT...?
Napoleon's mother liked to use Brocciu cheese in cooking and baking. The name of the cheese is derived from Corsican *brousser*, "to beat," a fact which indicates the thorough mixing process which occurs during the preparation of the cheese. In outlying mountain villages, this cheese provided a vital source of protein during the winter months.

PURCHASE/STORAGE:
Brocciu can be found only in specialized cheese shops. The best time for this cheese is from October to June. When you visit Corsica, do not forget to try this cheese. The cheese matures after several days in a vegetable box in a refrigerator.

Cabrales

Milk:

Country of origin:
Spain

Recommended drink:
Red wine,
e.g. Rioja

■ TYPE: Semi-hard, sliced cheese with blue rind

■ ORIGIN AND EXTENT: The Cabrales cheese is exclusively produced in the village of the same name and in three other villages in east Asturia in northern Spain.

■ FEATURES: Cabrales has a soft, cream-like consistency and is penetrated with gray-blue, narrow veins. The cheese has a cylindrical shape with a sticky, brown to black rind. Its weight ranges between 2.2 and 7 lb. The cheese is packed in a special dark green aluminum foil stamped with the impression of its origin to distinguish it from copies.

■ PRODUCTION: Cabrales is usually produced from raw cow's milk in the spring and summer. Goat and sheep's milk are added to cow's milk to produce this type of cheese. Whey and the lactic bacteria culture are added at low temperatures during the thickening process. The cheese is then cut into small pieces and pressed in cylindrical forms. Salt is added and the cheese is dried in the open air for one to two weeks. The proper maturation process begins when Cabrales is stored in humid limestone caves for at least 3 months.

IN THE KITCHEN

AROMA:
Cabrales has an intense, piquant flavor

FAT CONTENT:
45% fat in dry mass.

USE:
Cabrales is easily melted and can be used in small amounts as aromatic ingredient in sauces, meat and vegetable dishes.

PURCHASE/STORAGE:
Cabrales can be found in cheese shops or in Spanish specialty shops and is sold throughout the whole year. The Cabrales with the most intense flavor can only be bought in late summer. It can be stored, well packed, in a closed box for several days in the vegetable box of a refrigerator.

DID YOU KNOW THAT...?
The mold on the surface of Cabrales results from a higher content of spores in air. The cultures are not added to this cheese, as is the case with many other cheeses with blue rind.

Caciocavallo

Milk:
🐄 🥛

Country of origin:
Italy

Recommended
drink:
Dessert wine, e.g.
Marsala

■ TYPE: Filata cheese

■ ORIGIN AND EXTENT: Caciocavallo is produced throughout southern Italy.

■ FEATURES: Caciocavallo has a rounded or conical shape with or without a tip. Its weight varies from 2.2 to 5½ lb. Its light brown or yellow rind is thin and smooth. The cheese curd is homogenous, compact with very small holes. The outside yellow color is more intense, while inside it is lighter.

■ PRODUCTION: Caciocavallo is produced from cow's milk, which is soured at 97° to 100°F with the addition of calf or goat rennet. When the mass reaches the required consistency, it is broken into hazelnut-sized pieces. During the period of maturation, lactic fermentation occurs, which may last for a long or short period of time depending on the degree of the milk's acidity, temperature and mass. At a suitable moment, the cheese becomes elongated (filatura) and the curd is put into the demanded form. Finished cheese are cooled in water and then in salt brine. The cheese curd must remain in the brine for at least 6 hours. Then the cheese are bound in pairs and are hung for at least 15 days.

IN THE KITCHEN

AROMA:

Caciocavallo is aromatic, agreeable, and usually mild. Aged cheese has a delicious, piquant flavor.

FAT CONTENT:

38% fat in dry mass.

USE:

Young Caciocavallo is eaten as antipasta or on bread. The older the cheese, the less suitable it is for direct consumption. It is then used primarily for grating.

PURCHASE/STORAGE:

Caciocavallo can be found in cheese shops or in Italian specialty shops. It can be stored, well packed, in the vegetable box of a refrigerator.

DID YOU KNOW THAT...?

During the preparation of Cacio-cavallo, the cheese curd is mixed with water in a special type of mixer until the elastic mass is created. The mass is then elongated and put into called mold (in a process called "filature,") and finally bound with cord.

Camembert de Normandie

Milk:
🐄 🥛

Country of origin:
France

Recommended
drink:
Red wine,
e.g. fruity
Beaujolais

■ TYPE: Soft cheese with white rind

■ ORIGIN AND EXTENT: For many people, Camembert de Normandie is the quintessential French cheese. Before receiving the AOC-impression in 1983, it was the most imitated cheese throughout the world. The original cheese has the affix "de Normandie" in the name of the cheese. It can be produced only in Normandy by a precisely defined production method.

■ FEATURES: Camembert de Normandie has a round shape and a diameter that ranges from 4½ in with a height of 1 in. It weighs around 9 oz and is packed in a wooden box. The cheese has a very fine rind, covered with white mold, which may also have red spots on the surface.

■ PRODUCTION: Camembert de Normandie is prepared from raw cow's milk. After the addition of rennet, the milk is soured for 1 to 1½ hours. The sour is removed from whey with a perforated ladle. The cheese is then put into a mold and the remaining whey is left to drain. Salt is added and the cheeses are dried in "Héloir," a room with controlled temperature and humidity. The cheese matures in cellar for at least 21 days and is turned over every 24 hours.

■ HISTORICAL NOTE: According to legend, Camembert was invented during the French Rrevolution by country-woman named Marie Harel with the help of the insurgent priest whom she hid in her yard. Napoléon III was the greatest lover of Camembert and the cheese was served in his court. In 1880, engineer Ridel got the idea to pack it into a box made from thin wood, thus enabling the cheese to be transported long distances. This eventually led to its exportation.

■ OTHER CAMEMBERTS: *The German version of Camembert,* produced from pasteurized milk, is similar to the original. It weighs between 3 and 14 oz and reaches maturity within 8 to 10 days. The most well-known brands are Rotkäppchen and Champignon.

■ GOAT CAMEMBERT: Camembert produced from goat's milk is increasingly popular, especially as an organic cheese or a regional specialty.

Fried Camembert

■ INGREDIENTS: 1–2 Camemberts each weighing 8 oz • flour • 1 egg • sunflower oil • 1 bunch of fern parsley • ½ cup cowberry jam

■ PREPARATION: Divide the cheese into quarters and then spread flour over the surface. Coat the pieces of cheese with flour and eggs. Fry in hot oil until golden. Then drain the oil onto paper. Fry the parsley in oil. Remove from oil and allow to drain. Serve the pieces of cheese with parsley and cranberry jam.

IN THE KITCHEN

AROMA:
Young Camembert has a slightly sour flavor. Matured cheese has a mushroom flavor.

FAT CONTENT:
45% fat in dry mass.

USE:
Camembert de Normandie is well suited not only for serving sliced with farmer's bread, but it can be part of a cheese plate after a heavy meal. It can improve the flavor of soufflé and enhances dishes made from potatoes and vegetables. A classical element of Bavarian cuisine is pickled Camembert, known as Obatzer. Fried and roasted Camembert are also very popular.

PURCHASE/STORAGE:
Camembert de Normandie can only be obtained in specialized cheese shops. Camembert based on goat's milk can be found in eco shops.

Camemberts produced industrially can be stored at 50°F in a refrigerator. Handmade Camemberts matured to optimal flavor should be consumed on the day of purchase or 1 to 2 days after.

Cantal

Milk:
🐄 🥛

Country of origin:
France

Recommended
drink:
Red wine,
e.g. fruity Côtes
du Rhône
or Corbiéres

■ TYPE: Sliced cheese

■ ORIGIN AND EXTENSION: Cantal is a sliced cheese from Pays Vert, in the middle of Auvergne. This cheese has carried the AOC-impression since 1956. It is produced throughout the department of Canal and in 41 villages in the departments of Aveyron, Corréze, Haute-Loire and Puy-de-Dôme.

■ FEATURES: Cantal has a thick, dry, gray rind. The older the cheese, the stronger and more golden yellow the rind. During the early stages of its maturation, the consistency is firm and soft and in the mature stage it is brittle. Cantal is cylindrical with a diameter of 16 in, a height of 18 in and weighs about 95 lbs. Sometimes a smaller version is produced, known as "Petit Cantal." It weighs only 40 lbs. Even smaller is "Cantalet," which weighs 20 lbs.

■ PRODUCTION: Cantal is produced from fermented cow's milk. The curd is mixed, pressed and following the period of maturation, it is cut up again into smaller pieces. Then salt is added to the cheese, the cheese is formed and pressed for 48 hours. The formed cheese matures for at least 30 days in a cellar. The mature Cantal is stored 4 to 6 months.

IN THE KITCHEN

AROMA:
Young Cantal has a slightly sour and bitter flavor. Mature Cantal is expressive and piquant.

FAT CONTENT:
45% fat in dry mass.

USE:
Cantal is well suited for fruits. Thanks to its good melting qualities, it is suitable for cooking. It is possible to use it in the preparation of soufflé and gratinated dishes, as well as in soups and sauces, where the cheese provides an agreeable spicy flavor.

PURCHASE/STORAGE:
Cantal can only be bought in cheese shops. It should be stored in the vegetable box of a refrigerator for several weeks, packed in grease-proof paper and perforated aluminum foil.

Chabichou du Poitou

Milk:
🐐 🥛

Country of origin:
France

Recommended
drink:
White wine,
e.g. Sancerre

TYPE: Soft cheese

ORIGIN AND EXTENT: Chabichou du Poitou comes from the limestone region Haut-Poitou in western France, a region which includes Vienne, Deux-Sèvres and Charente.

FEATURES: Chabichou du Poitou has the characteristic shape of a truncated cone with a height of 2½ in, a diameter 2 to 2½ in and weighs about 5 oz. The curd has a fine consistency. When the cheese matures, the curd is more firm and friable. Its fine rind has white or blue mold on the surface.

PRODUCTION: Chabichou du Poitou is produced exclusively from goat's milk. The milk is treated with whey. The curd is left to drain on cloth and a ladle is used to put it into molds. After the formation process and the adding of salt, the cheese is placed in a drying room where it matures for at least 10 days.

OTHER CHABICHOU CHEESES: Besides Chabichou du Poitou, a bearer of the AOC-impression, numerous variants exist, all of which have a cylindrical shape.

IN THE KITCHEN

AROMA:
Chabichou du Poitou has slightly goatish, mildly acidic flavor. As it matures, the flavor grows stronger, but not sharper. It has a slightly goatish smell.

FAT CONTENT:
45% fat in dry mass.

USE:
Chabichou du Poitou is usually bought in one piece and enhances any cheese plate.

PURCHASE/STORAGE:
Chabichou du Poitou is a rarity. The most suitable time of purchase is from late spring to early autumn. Other sorts of Chabichous can be bought more often. This cheese can be stored for a short time in one piece well packed in the vegetable box of a refrigerator.

DID YOU KNOW THAT...?
According to legend Chabichou du Poitou descended from the 8th century from Arabian tribes – the Saracens. Chabi, the abbreviation of Chabichou, may be derived from "chebli," the Persian word for goat.

Chaource

Milk:
🐄 🥛

Country of origin:
France

Recommended
drink:
White wine, e.g.
Chablis,
Champagne, or
also red burgundy

■ TYPE: Soft cheese with white rind

■ ORIGIN AND EXTENT: The crade of this famous cheese, named after a village called Chaorce, lies in the northeastern part of France. Other places of Chaource production include the areas of Aube and Yonne in Burgundy, which according to AOC, are permitted to produce this protected cheese.

■ FEATURES: This young cheese has a firm and crumbly core which becomes supple after maturation. The rind is covered by fine, white mold. The cheese is available in two sizes: the large Chaource has a diameter of 4 in, a height 2 in and weighs about 1 lb. The smaller variant has a diameter of 3 in and weighs only 7 oz.

■ PRODUCTION: When rennet is added to cow's milk, it sours within 24 hours. The curd is then poured into round, perforated molds. The cheese mass does not have a fixed bottom, so the whey can slowly drain. The salting and drying is done on straw beds and the cheese matures after fifteen days.

IN THE KITCHEN

AROMA:
Young Chaource has a light acidulous flavor. The matured cheese has a fruity and slightly nutty flavor.

FAT CONTENT:
50% fat in dry mass.

USE:
Chaource harmonizes especially well with grapes and can be served with an aperitif. It is very good roasted and served with fresh salad. The mature Chaource can be offered to cheese lovers for dessert.

DID YOU KNOW THAT...?

As early as the fourteenth century, this cheese was prepared in Champagne.

PURCHASE/STORAGE:
Chaource can only be found in cheese shops. The best quality is available in summer and fall. It should be consumed immediately, but it can also be stored in the vegetable box of a refrigerator. If storing, pack it with grease-proof paper in a plastic box.

Cheddar

Milk:

Country of origin:
Great Britain

Recommended drink:
White wine, e.g. gray burgundy

■ TYPE: Sliced cheese

■ ORIGIN AND EXTENT: The most popular British cheese comes from county of Somerset in southwest England. It got its name because it originated from a town of the same name.

■ FEATURES: Traditionally, the cheese is cylinder-shaped and weighs 55 lb with a diameter of 16 in and a height of 16 in. It is currently produced in the form of 4 lb blocks and wheels. The curd of the cheese is light yellow or orange and has a firm consistency. The rind is thin and yellow or brown, depending on its maturation time.

■ PRODUCTION: The cheese was first made in the 16th century and was produced industrially by the middle of the 19th century. After souring and draining cow's milk, the cheese is cut into pieces of manageable size. These pieces are arranged side by side, allowing better draining of the whey, an arrangement called "cheddaring" which gives a special consistency to the dough. Cheddar of excellent quality is stored at least 9 months to 2 years, depending on the quality, but it can be sold after 3 months. This type of Cheddar is quite common.

■■■ HISTORICAL NOTE: Cheddar was formerly a farmer cheese. Depending on the wealth of the farmer, the cheese was prepared from whole milk or from skimmed milk. The fatless cheese was a lighter color and it was sometimes necessary to imitate the color of whole milk cheddar by adding saffron, or later annatto, in order to sell it.

■■■ VARIANTS OF CHEDDAR: *Farmhouse Cheddar* is traditionally prepared in small amounts and matures for at least 14 months. It is named the "King of Cheddar."

Sage Derby: During cheddaring, sage leaves are added. The cheese thus obtains green striping and has a strong herbal flavor.

Aromatic Cheddar: Besides traditional Sage Derby, Cheddar can be aromatized with beer, whisky, port wine or chili. The scent of these ingredients can be considered agreeable or disturbing according to individual taste.

Five Counties: This cheese is offered in 2 lb rounds. It is a mixture of five types of English cheese. After the maturation phase, five layers can be seen inside: Cheddar (light yellow), Leicester (rich yellow), Cheshire (white), Double Gloucester (gold yellow) and Derby (yellow).

HAVE YOU TRIED...?

Cheese soufflé: Mix 4 oz grated Cheddar and 4 yolks with cool Béchamel sauce, add 4 beaten whites and put it all in the mold. Let it bake at 392°F for about 25 minutes. Serve immediately. White Côtes du Rhône is well suited for this dish.

IN THE KITCHEN

AROMA:
Cheddar has an aromatic, slightly nutty flavor, the piquancy of which ranges from mild to strong according to the stage of maturity.

FAT CONTENT:
50% fat in dry mass.

USE:
There is a great variety of uses for Cheddar. According to English tradition, it is eaten with some crackers and pieces of celery, but it also complements fruit and can be used in sandwiches or in soufflés.

> DID YOU KNOW THAT...?
> It is an English custom to offer red wine or a glass of liqueur with old Cheddar.

PURCHASE/STORAGE:
Cheddar can be found anywhere, but traditional English Cheddar can only be bought in cheese shops. The best way to store this cheese is alone, or with cheeses of the same type, packed in grease-proof paper in the refrigerator. It can be stored for a very long time.

Cheshire

Milk:
🐄 🥛

Country of origin:
Great Britain

Recommended
drink:
White wine, e.g.
Riesling

▬ TYPE: Sliced cheese

▬ ORIGIN AND EXTENT: Perhaps the oldest cheese of England and probably Celtic in origin, Cheshire comes from the county of Westchester on the Welsh border. The cheese is also known as Chester.

▬ FEATURES: Traditionally round, this cheese weighs about 49 lb, it has a diameter of 12 in and the height is 14 in. It is currently produced in the shape of blocks or wheels. The almost white dough has a rough texture and the rind is yellow brown.

▬ PRODUCTION: Cheshire cheese is produced from the milk of cows pastured in meadows. It has a mild salt content. Traditionally, the pressed curd was packed into cloth and set aside to mature for at least 3 to 6 months.

▬ VARIANT OF CHESHIRE: *Shropshire blue* is a Cheshire cheese colored with annatto to which the culture of Stilton was added. The curd is blue striped and has a pungent aroma.

In the kitchen

Aroma:
Cheshire has a piquant, slightly salty, spicy flavor.

Fat content:
50% fat in dry mass.

Use:
Formerly it was the British custom to offer Cheshire cheese with fruit cake. However, it is also very nice with pears or apples. It is suitable for toast and also for cooking. An omelet is enhanced with a little Cheshire cheese.

Purchase/storage:
Cheshire (or Chester) cheese can be found anywhere, but can be difficult to distinguish from Cheddar. Proper English Cheshire can be bought in specialized cheese shops.
It is best to refrigerate this cheese with cheeses of the same type, packed with grease-proof paper in a plastic box.

Chevrotin

Milk:
🐐 🥛

Country of origin:
France

Recommended
drink:
Red wine from
Savoy, e.g.
Abymes

■ TYPE: Semi-hard, sliced cheese

■ ORIGIN AND EXTENT: Chevrotin originated in Savoy, in the region of Rhônes-Alpes. Since May 2002, the family crest has been imprinted side by side with the AOC impression.

■ FEATURES: Chevrotin has a red brown rind and soft white yellow dough. The cheese has a flat, cylindrical shape with a diameter of 3½ to 5 in and a height of 1 to 2 in. Its weight ranges between 9 to 12 oz.

■ PRODUCTION: Only the raw milk of goats that pasture in the summer on mountain hayfields rich in herbs and feed on hay in the winter may be used for the production of Chevrotin. The production is manual in all stages. Chevrotin matures for at least 3 weeks on spruce wood and three times per week it is turned over and washed with brine.

■ HISTORICAL NOTICE: Chevrotin has been known since the 17th century. The translation of its name is "little goat." Specialists consider this cheese a younger brother of Reblochon.

IN THE KITCHEN

AROMA:
Chevrotin has a mellow, slightly acidic flavor reminiscent of wild herbs.

FAT CONTENT:
45% fat in dry mass.

USE:
The cheese is ideal for breakfast sandwiches, but nicely complements other cheese types on a cheese plate after the main course.

PURCHASE/STORAGE:
Sometimes you can find Chevrotin in specialized cheese shops. It can be stored for a short time packed with grease-proof paper and closed in a plastic case in the vegetable box of a refrigerator.

Comté

Milk:

Country of origin:
France
Recommended
drink:
Light red and dry
white wine from
Côtes du Jura

■ TYPE: Hard cheese

■ ORIGIN AND EXTENT: Comté mountain cheese originated in French Jura, a region is known for its lush, green mountain pastures and hay fields, where the Montbéliard and Pie-Rouge cows pasture. Only the milk of these two breeds is used for the production of Comté cheese.

■ FEATURES: The curd of Comté cheese is compact and smooth. The surface is grainy and may have a gold yellow color. The margin has a slightly convex shape and its height is 3½ to 5 in. The weight of the cheese is 66 to 121 lb. Each cheese is checked by the Appellation Committee before it is placed on the market. If approved, the sign of the green tree is imprinted on the margin of the cheese or on the case.

■ PRODUCTION: Comté is produced from partially skimmed, raw milk. The milk must be processed for 24 hours. The curd is cut up into small pieces and heated about 45 minutes at 129°F while stirring and then pressed for 20 hours. The cheese is formed intowheels, salted and turned regularly. After about 3 months of maturation, the cheese can be sold.

IN THE KITCHEN

AROMA:
Comté is a very aromatic cheese. It is prepared from summer milk and has a more pronounced flavor than lighter colored cheese made from winter milk, which is marked by a nutty flavor.

FAT CONTENT:
45% fat in dry mass.

USE:
It may seem unusual, but the cheese is well suited for fish and seafood. Comté can also be served with an aperitif at the end of the meal.

PURCHASE/STORAGE:
Comté can occasionally be bought in supermarkets and is usually found in specialized cheese shops. To store it, wrap in grease-proof paper and perforated aluminum foil.

DID YOU KNOW THAT...?
The cheese in the Comté region has been produced for more than 1,000 years. The cheese was a reliable source of food for people over long winters.

Crottin de Chavignol

Milk:

Country of origin:
France

Recommended
drink:
White wine, e.g.
Sancerre or
Pouilly-Fumé

■ TYPE: Soft cheese

■ ORIGIN AND EXTENT: The origin of Crottin de Chavignol lies south of middle Loire, in the departments Cher, Loiret and Nièvre.

■ FEATURES: Crottin de Chavignol is a small round cheese with a slightly rounded margin. Its white, compact dough is surrounded by a fine, natural mold rind. The loaf of cheese weighs about 2 oz and is sold unpacked.

■ PRODUCTION: Crottin de Chavignol is produced from goat's milk with a small amount of whey. The curd is drained on linen cloth and is filled into special molds called "Faisselles." The cheese is then dried and during the drying, it is often turned over. The cheese matures for at least 10 days.

■ HISTORICAL NOTE: It is known that the farmers around Sancerre raised goats and obtained the cheese from the milk. The cheese was the main source of their incomes.

IN THE KITCHEN

AROMA:
Crottin de Chavignol has a typical goat flavor, milder in summer and more intense in fall. Its smell is also mildly goat-like.

FAT CONTENT:
45% fat in dry mass.

USE:
Crottin de Chavignol is usually bought in one whole piece. It can be pickled in wine and herbs or in oil and herbs. Often the entire piece of cheese is grilled.

PURCHASE/STORAGE:
Crottin de Chavignol can be found in cheese shops. It can be stored for a short time, well wrapped, in the vegetable box of refrigerator.

DID YOU KNOW THAT...?

This cheese obtained its name as late as in the year of 1829. *Crottin* is the name for small oil lamps that have the same shape as the cheese. The word also means "horse apple." It is assumed that the cheese obtained its name due to its particular shape.

Edam

Milk:

Country of origin:
Netherlands

Recommended
drink:
Beer, e.g. Pilsner
or Export

▬ TYPE: Sliced cheese

▬ ORIGIN AND EXTEN: Edam obtained its name from the small harbor town on Ijsselmeer, north of Amsterdam. Formerly this cheese was produced in the northern part of the province of Holland. Today it is produced not only throughout the Netherlands, but also in Germany and other middle and north European countries.

▬ FEATURES: The cheese has the shape of a sphere with a diameter of 5 in and weighs about 3 lb. The curd is golden yellow, the holes are small and the consistency is firm. The cheese is traditionally covered by a red layer of paraffin wast, which protects it against drying up.

▬ PRODUCTION: Edam is usually produced from pasteurized, partially skimmed cow's milk. After the whey has been drained and the cheese formed, salted and pressed, it matures for at least one month.

IN THE KITCHEN

AROMA:
Edam has a mild to slightly piquant, salty flavor.

FAT CONTENT:
40% fat in dry mass.

USE:
Edam is a typical breakfast cheese. It is well-suited for either toast or black bread. It harmonizes excellently with tomato, cucumber or paprika. Due to its low fat content, it is not a good melting cheese.

Purchase/storage:
Edam can be found in supermarkets packed in foil. No cheese stand is complete without this cheese. It is advantageous to buy it in one whole piece because it does not dry out quickly. At home, the cheese should be stored in the refrigerator. It is best when the cheese is stored alone or with cheeses of the same type, wrapped in grease-proof paper in a plastic box.

OTHER SORTS:
German Edam is produced according to the Dutch model. Even 11 lb blocks are available and it should mature for 5 weeks.

Emmentaler

Milk:
🐄 🥛

Country of origin:
Switzerland

Recommended
drink:
Red wine, e.g.
late burgundy

TYPE: Hard cheese

ORIGIN AND EXTENT: The home of this cheese is the valley of the Emme River in the canton of Bern. The cheese is produced mostly in the Emme valley, but also throughout German speaking Switzerland.

FEATURES: The round, arched cheeses have heights of 7 to 10 in and diameters of 30 to 37 in. One loaf weighs 154 to 265 lbs. Emmentaler is famous for its holes and its nutty flavor. Its light yellow curd is mild and supple. The rind is firm, dry and yellow-brown.

PRODUCTION: Emmentaler is produced from the raw milk of hay-fed cows. The raw milk is heated in copper kettles and diluted with the whey. The pieces of curd are broken to smaller pieces and heated again while stirring. Then the cheese mass is put into molds and pressed. After the cheese is formed, salt is added. The cheese matures for at least 120 days.

HISTORICAL NOTE: This cheese was first documented in 1542. It was used as compensation for victims of a catastrophic fire.

OTHER SORTS: Like the Swiss original, *Allgäuer Emmentaler* must mature for 3 months and is also produced from raw milk. Another version of Emmentaler produced in Germany is made of pasteurized milk and its time of maturity is 2 months. This cheese is then known as "Emmentaler," followed by its place of production and should not be mistaken for the original Emmentaler.

Emmentaler "matured in cave" matures up to 18 months and has an intense, nutty aroma.

Gratinated asparagus

INGREDIENTS: • 2 lb green asparagus • salt • 1 tablespoon butter • 1 pinch sugar • 1 lemon • 2 oz butter • 1 bunch of parsley • salt and pepper • 1 lb mushrooms • 1 red paprika • 5 oz boiled ham • 5 oz Emmentaler

PREPARATION: Wash the asparagus, remove woody parts. Then boil it with 1 quart water in large pot with salt, sugar and butter and two lemon slices. Asparagus should be boiled about 8–10 minutes until it can be bitten through. Preheat the oven to 392°F. Let the asparagus thoroughly drain

and combine with 2 oz hot butter, add salt, pepper and parsley. Stew 1 lb thinly sliced mushrooms with butter. Add paprika, cut into small pieces, and then stew the mixture again. Cut the ham into small cubes. Put asparagus, champignons and paprika in layers into a buttered soufflé mold. Spread with grated Emmentaler and gratinate 15 to 20 minutes at 356°F.

IN THE KITCHEN

AROMA:
Emmentaler has a fine, slightly nutty, almost saltless flavor.

FAT CONTENT:
45% fat in dry mass.

USE:
Emmentaler is used for cold as well as hot dishes. Its good melting qualities mean it is used for baking vegetable and potatoes dishes. Piquant pastry has a finer flavor. Emmentaler is also used as cubed cheese or for canapés.

PURCHASE/STORAGE:
Emmentaler can be found in any large cheese stand. The cheese should be stored in the refrigerator, alone or with the cheeses of the same type, wrapped in grease-proof paper and perforated aluminum foil.

Epoisses de Bourgogne

Milk:

Country of origin:
France

Recommended
drink:
White wine, e.g.
gray burgundy,
but also sweet
wines or Marc de
Bourgogne

▬ TYPE: Soft cheese with washed rind

▬ ORIGIN AND EXTENT: Epoisses originates from Burgundy; departments Côte d'Or, Yonne and Haute-Marne.

▬ FEATURES: The orange-red surface results from the growth of red cultures. The dough is light beige, supple and soft. Epoisses occurs in two different sizes: A cylinder with a 4 to 4½ in diameter has a 1 to 2 in height and a weight of 9 to 12 oz. A cylinder of Epoisses with a diameter of 6½ to 7½ in has the same height, but a weight of 1½ to 2 lb.

▬ PRODUCTION: Epoisses is produced from cow's milk, which is soured by adding lactic acid bacteria. The delicate curd crumbles quickly so it must be carefully formed. The cheese matures for at least 4 weeks. During its maturation, the cheese is washed one to three times per week with salty water and with Marc de Bourgogne, the brandy made from burgundy. The concentration of brandy used for washing is increased during the maturation process.

In the kitchen

Aroma:
Epoisses has a strong, pungent flavor. Marc de Bourgogne is considered to have a delicately alcoholic aroma.

Fat content:
50% fat in dry mass.

Use:
Epoisses is best suited as the last course of the meal. To enjoy its extraordinary taste best, combine it with a fresh baguette. Epoisses is not suitable for warm dishes.

Purchase/storage:
Epoisses can be found in cheese shops. Once it is cut, it should be eaten. It does not keep well, even in the refrigerator. If you must store it, wrap the cheese in grease-proof paper and keep in a tightly closed box.

Did you know that...?
According to legend, Epoisses was invented by Cistercian monks in the early 16th century. More likely it came from peasant women, who improved upon the old method of producing the cheese and handed it down from mother to daughter. The theory is confirmed by finding stones for draining, as well as drying rooms and cellars for mature cheeses, in farmhouses around Epoisses before the 19th century.

Esrom

Milk:
🐄 🥛

Country of origin:
Denmark

Recommended drink: Beer, e.g. Altbier

■ TYPE: Sliced cheese

■ ORIGIN AND EXTENT: The origin of Esrom is the Danish island of Seeland. The cheese was produced there for a long time as a monastery cheese and then completely forgotten. Around 1930, this method of preparation was newly invented and the process was optimized. Today, it is produced all over Denmark and protected by a European Union statement of origin.

■ FEATURES: Esrom has rectangular, flat body, with a weight range from 7 oz to 4 lbs. The curd is pale yellow, very soft and shows small, irregularly situated holes. It has a thin, straw-colored rind.

■ PRODUCTION: Esrom is produced from pasteurized cow's milk. The milk is soured by adding rennet, the curd is cut up into small pieces, placed into molds and lightly pressed. After adding salt, the cheese matures at least 4 weeks.

IN THE KITCHEN

AROMA:
Young Esrom has a mild spicy flavor.

FAT CONTENT:
45% fat in dry mass.

USE:
In Denmark, Esrom is consumed mainly with bread, tomatoes and cucumbers. Its strong variant is suitable when creating a cheese plate.

PURCHASE/STORAGE:
Wrapped Esrom can be found in discount food stores, supermarkets and cheese stands as well as cheese shops. At home, the cheese should be stored in a tightly closed case in the vegetable box of the refrigerator, wrapped in greaseproof paper.

Feta

Milk:

Country of origin:
Greece

Recommended
drink:
White wine, e.g.
Roditis

TYPE: Soft cheese

ORIGIN AND EXTENT: Feta has been produced in Greece since antiquity and its production has spread all over the Balkans. Feta became a cheese of protected origin in 2002 and after a period of 5 years it will only be produced in Greece. (Most of the Feta consumed in Germany comes from Denmark and Germany.) According to European Union regulations, only sheep and goat's milk may be used for its production. But today, Feta is produced mostly from cow's milk.

FEATURES: The name of the cheese comes from Greek word fetas, which means "disc." Feta has no rind and has a firm consistency. Its color is white and is stored in brine or in whey.

PRODUCTION: Feta of protected origin is usually made from sheep's milk. It is possible to add goat's milk to the production process, but the same is not true for cow's milk. The milk is diluted with whey and put into perforated wooden or thin metal molds. The curd is pressed for 24 hours and the whey is left to drain. After that, the curd is cut up into pieces and stored in steel tanks filled with brine. Then it is tightly packed with a small amount of brine, and sold.

▬ HISTORICAL NOTE: Until the 19th century, the farmers and shepherds in Mani (on Peloponnes) poured the milk into vessels. Thanks to the remaining remnants of cheese, there was enough bacteria and whey to sour the milk. Alternatively, the sap obtained from fig twigs or thistle flowers was used as well. Then the curd was pressed and the disks of cheese were put in wooden barrels filled with brine. The further the distance the cheese had to be transported, the more salt was added.

Feta and Tomato Omelet

▬ INGREDIENTS: 3 tomatoes • 2 tablespoons butter • 5 eggs • salt with herbs • pepper • leaves of Basil • 7 tablespoons Feta

▬ PREPARATION: Pare the tomatoes, cut them into quarters and remove the seeds, then cut them into small cubes. Stew the tomatoes in a small amount of butter for about 5 minutes. Beat the eggs with the salt and pepper. Prepare two omelets on the frying pan. Put the finished omelet on a plate, add the tomatoes and the small pieces of cheese, fold the omelet in two and decorate with basil.

Shepherd salad

▬ INGREDIENTS: 1 small iceberg salad • 1 pickle • 5 tomatoes • 1 red pepper • 1 onion • 2 tablespoons of olive oil • the juice of 1 lemon • salt and pepper • Feta • black olives

▬ PREPARATION: Clean and cut the vegetables. Mix everything together. With the oil, lemon juice, salt and pepper prepare a vinaigrette dressing, pour it on the salad, add the black olives and the cheese cut into small cubes. Serve with rye bread.

IN THE KITCHEN

AROMA:
Feta has a salty, slightly acidulous flavor. It often smells like acid milk.

FAT CONTENT:
45% fat in dry mass.

USE:
Feta is the favorite cheese in Greek and Turkish cuisines. It is always present in farmer's salad, where it is combined with tomatoes. It is also consumed crumbled and baked in many piquant Greek cakes.

PURCHASE/STORAGE:
Feta can be found on cooled shelves in any supermarket. It can be bought in any Turkish shop. Once open, it can be kept for 1 to 2 days in the refrigerator.

Fontina

Milk:
🐄 🍼

Country of origin:
Italy

Recommended
drink:
Red wine, e.g.
Barbaresco

TYPE: Semi-hard, sliced cheese

ORIGIN AND EXTENT: Fontina comes from the Aosta valley in northwest Italy near the Swiss and French Alps.

FEATURES: Fontina is a flat, round cheese with slightly concave margin. The height is 3 to 4 in, with a diameter of 12 to 18 in and a weight range of 18 to 40 lbs. Its firm rind is only 2 mm thick. The straw-colored curd is soft and elastic with very small holes.

PRODUCTION: Fontina is produced from a single milking and ferments due to a natural degree of acidity. The cheese from raw milk is salted as dry. The cheese matures for about 3 months in rooms with a temperature of 43° to 50°F and 90% humidity.

VARIANT: Fontal. This cheese is prepared similarly to Fontina. Its large area of production includes some regions in France. Its flavor is usually less aromatic than the original cheese.

IN THE KITCHEN

AROMA:

Fontina is a mild aromatic cheese which melts readily.

FAT CONTENT:

45% fat in dry mass.

USE:

In its country, Fontina is spread on bread for brunch. Fonduta is a Piedmontese variant of Swiss fondue. Due to its fine melting qualities, Fontina is used in the preparation of many dishes.

PURCHASE/STORAGE:

Fontina can be bought in specialized cheese shops or in an Italian specialty shops. It should be kept, well wrapped, in the vegetable box of the refrigerator.

Fourme d'Ambert

Milk:

Country of origin:
France

Recommended
drink:
Red wine, e.g.
Côtes du Rhône,
or Riesling from
Alsatia

■ TYPE: Sliced cheese with inner mold

■ ORIGIN AND EXTENT: The home of Fourme d'Ambert lies in Auvergne in central France. The production is limited to the departments of Loire and Puy-de-Dôme and five cantons of Cantal in the surrounding area of Saint-Flour.

■ FEATURES: At first glance, this tall and broad cheese is different from other cheeses. The cylinder has a diameter of 5 in and a height of about 8 in. The surface is ochre-colored and slightly red. The curd is almost gray and is streaked with thick blue veins. Fourme d'Ambert weighs about 4 lbs.

■ PRODUCTION: The cow's milk is heated and soured by means of rennet. It is then cut up, stirred and then manually poured into forms, inoculated by blue mold and salted. The cheese is frequently turned over during the whey drying process. To support the development of the mold, the inside of the cheese is perforated, allowing many air channels to form. The period of maturation is at least 28 days.

■ HISTORICAL NOTICE: The word "fourme" is derived from Latin *forma*, or 'form.' It is said that all French cheeses originate in Auvergne. Some people claim that the inhabitants

of Auvergne produced Fourme d'Ambert before the conquest by Julius Caesar. There is written evidence of the production of this cheese dating back to the 8th century. Formerly, Fourme was produced in so-called "Jasseries," which combine a farmyard with a dairy.

■■■ OTHER VARIATIONS OF FOURME WITH AOC-IMPRESSION: *Fourme de Montbrison*. Since 2002, the Montbrison has had its own AOC-impression. Its aroma is very fine and slightly nutty. It is an ideal cheese for novice cheese connoisseurs who want to increase their enjoyment of blue cheese gradually.

Mixed salad with fresh figs

■■■ INGREDIENTS: 7 oz mixed salad • 9 oz fresh figs • 7 oz Fourme d'Ambert • 2–3 tablespoons Sherry vinegar • 4 tablespoons grape seed oil • pinch of sugar • salt • milled black pepper

■■■ PREPARATION: Clean and drain salad. Wash the figs and divide them into 8 portions. Cut the Fourme d'Ambert into small cubes. Arrange salad, figs and cheese on 4 plates. Prepare the dressing by mixing the vinegar, oil, sugar, salt and pepper. Spread the dressing on the salad.

IN THE KITCHEN

AROMA:
Fourme d'Ambert has a nutty mushroom flavor. You will find that this cheese is milder than other cheeses with blue rind.

FAT CONTENT:
50% fat in dry mass.

USE:
Fourme is suitable for use in salads, soufflés and crêpes. Thanks to its fine taste, it is ideal for dishes requiring an unobtrusive, nutty, mushroom flavor.

PURCHASE/STORAGE:
You can find Fourme d'Ambert and Fourme de Montbrison in special cheese shops. The cheeses can be kept for several days wrapped in grease-proof paper and closed tightly in a case in the vegetable box of the refrigerator.

Gjetost

Milk:

Country of origin:
Norway

Recommended
drink: Aquavit

■ TYPE: Sliced cheese

■ ORIGIN AND EXTENT: Gjetost is a Norwegian national products and is also called "brown cheese." It is a crucial part of any traditional Norwegian cheese plate and is also known as Norgold.

■ FEATURES: Gjetost is a rectangular cheese without a rind. It is a caramel brown color with a firm consistency. Its weight ranges from 9 oz and 2 lbs. Before being sold, the cheese is wrapped in foil.

■ PRODUCTION: Traditionally, Gjetost is produced mostly from goat's milk whey. Today, the cheese is prepared from cow's milk whey combined with a little goat's milk whey. The whey is slowly boiled, three quarters of water is vaporize and the milk sugar becomes caramelized as the milk protein is soured. It is possible to add some milk and cream and thus to adjust the fat content and make the cheese more supple. The brown paste is salted and pressed into blocks. The cheese does not need to mature and may be packed immediately.

IN THE KITCHEN

AROMA:

Gjetost has a sweet, caramel, yet simultaneously salty, flavor.

FAT CONTENT:

35% fat in dry mass.

USE:

This cheese is eaten with jam for breakfast and can also be consumed as a dessert with fruit cake or fruits.

DID YOU KNOW THAT...?

Norway was already known for its export of butter in the 9th and 10th century. During butter production, large amounts of whey are produced as waste. Utilization of the leftover whey was the ideal result of cheese production. In many rich countries, the whey was used for feeding cattle. This was not possible in Norway where the winter is long and severe and the period of goat milking very short.

PURCHASE/STORAGE:

Gjetost is available in specialized cheese shops. It can be kept for several days well wrapped in the vegetable box of a refrigerator.

Ekte Gjetost made only from goat's milk is difficult to obtain.

Gorgonzola

Milk:
🐮 🥛

Country of origin:
Italy

Recommended
drink:
Red wine, e.g.
Barolo, or noble
sweet white wine

▬ TYPE: Soft blue cheese with rind

▬ ORIGIN AND EXTENT: Gorgonzola is produced in Lombardy and in Piedmont. The cheese obtained its name from the small Lombardi village north of Milan where the cheese was prepared 1,000 years ago.

▬ FEATURES: Gorgonzola has a cylindrical shape with a high, flat margin. Its height is 6 to 8 in, its diameter is 10 to 12 in and its weight ranges between 13 and 29 lbs. Its rind is rough and slightly reddish colored. The cheese is straw-colored and striped with green veins of mold.

▬ PRODUCTION: Gorgonzola is produced exclusively from full fat cow's milk, treated at 82° to 90°F with calf rennet and inoculated with spores of blue mold. After several days, it undergoes dry salting in rooms with a temperature of 64° to 68°F. Then the cheese matures for 2 or 3 months at a temperature of 41° to 46°F. During its maturation period, the curd is perforated several times to support the development of blue mold, characteristic of this type of cheese and giving it the green color of noble mold. At the end of the process, the cheese should be wrapped in aluminum foil or another protective material.

■ HISTORICAL NOTE: This cheese was invented by one Lombardy farmer who offered his guests some moldy pieces of cheese. The guests were delighted with this specialty and so the cheese with noble mold was born.

■ SPECIALTIES: *Torta Crema*, Gorgonzola with Mascarpone, is a small cylinder, in which two types of cheese were arranged in layers to form a cake. This specialty is often referred to as creamy Gorgonzola. It has a mild flavor, but a short shelf life due to the combination of two types of cheese. *Dolcelatte (Pronunciation: Doltche Latte)* is the trade name for a very fine creamy Gorgonzola. Its maturation period is shorter and it is less penetrated with the veins of mold.

Filled omelet

■ INGREDIENTS: 2 eggs • 3½ tablespoons butter • 7 table-spoons flour • salt • 1 tablespoon butter • 1 tablespoon flour • 3 cups milk • 1 lb spinach • 1 onion • 1 tablespoon butter • 5 oz Gorgonzola

■ PREPARATION: Beat eggs with 2 tablespoons butter and milk, add the flour, salt and let it rest for 30 minutes. To prepare a béchamel, melt one tablespoon butter, add the flour and the milk while stirring and heat slightly. Stir until mixture becomes smooth. Let boil for 5 minutes and then add pepper and salt. Clean and wash the spinach, put it into a pot and allow it to stew for 5 minutes. Then remove it from the water and cut roughly. Stew the minced onion with butter, add the spinach and Gorgonzola mixed with small amount of béchamel. Then spread the spinach on the omelet, put it in a soufflé dish, cover with béchamel and bake in the oven at 428°F.

IN THE KITCHEN

AROMA:

The young Gorgonzola is called "dolce" or "sweet." When the cheese ages, however, it loses its sweet flavor and aquires a spicy, piquant taste. The matured cheese is named "piquant" and has a stronger, more acidulous flavor.

FAT CONTENT:

48% fat in dry mass.

USE:

Gorgonzola with black olives and radishes is delicious. It is offered also with walnuts and mixed lettuce salad. Gorgonzola is traditionally combined with spinach as omelet filling. The famous cheese cannot be omitted when composing an Italian cheese plate.

PURCHASE/STORAGE:

Gorgonzola can be found in any well-supplied cheese stand. It can be kept for several days in a sealed case in the vegetable box of a refrigerator.

DID YOU KNOW THAT...?

Formerly Gorgonzola was filled with warm, sour milk of the morning and the cool sour of the evening was added later.

Gouda

Milk:

Country of origin:
Netherlandes

Recommened
drink: Pilsner
beer or Export

TYPE: Sliced cheese

ORIGIN AND EXTENT: Gouda is the most important Dutch cheese. It comes from the small town of Gouda, northeast of Rotterdam. By the Middle Ages, the cheese was exported outside Netherlands and it became a delicacy for Englishmen as well as for the whole of northeastern Europe.

FEATURES: The cheese is shaped like a cartwheel with a diameter of 12 in. It is covered by a yellow plastic layer. The younger the cheese, the lighter its color. It has a supple, but firm consistency. Due to the loss of water during the long period of maturation, the rind becomes thicker and the cheese firmer.

INGREDIENTS: Unless otherwise stated, Gouda cheese is composed of pasteurized cow's milk. Formally, Gouda was made from raw milk. Since the Middle Ages, various spices have been added to Gouda to improve its aroma and to secure a greater durability. The most common include caraway seeds, pepper and various herbs.

CLASSICAL SORTS OF GOUDA:
Young cheese (Jong): The time of maturation is only 4 to 6 weeks. Children love this mild-flavored, light-colored cheese.

Middle-aged cheese (Belegen): This cheese is known as "Pikantje van Antje." Middle-aged cheese matures for 3 to 6 months and its color is darker with an agreeably piquant flavor.

Three-quarters old cheese (Extra-belegen): After 6 to 8 months this cheese is darker and has a strong aroma.

Old cheese (Oud): Gouda cheese is "old" if its time of maturation is between 8 months and 2 years. This cheese is then crumbly and has an almost orange yellow color. It is usually covered with black plastic. It is hard to slice and is very crumbly due to a small water content.

OTHER SORTS: Goat's milk Gouda. Gouda can even be obtained from goat's milk. This white cheese has a mild flavor. This cheese also occurs in a variety of ages and is usually improved by adding spices.

German Gouda: This cheese is produced according to the original Dutch formula.

Cheese hedgehog:

■■ INGREDIENTS: 1 grapefruit • 14 oz Gouda • radishes • cornichons (pickles) • baby corn ears • small sausages • cocktail cherries • pineapple chunks • mandarin oranges • grapes • toothpicks

■■ PREPARATION: Cut the cheese into small cubes and then cut the other ingredients into bite-sized pieces. Stick them on toothpicks, alternating with the cheese cubes, and stick into the grapefruit.

In the kitchen

Aroma:
The flavor of Gouda ranges from mild to and piquant spicy.

Fat content:
45% fast in dry mass.

Use:
Gouda is highly useful in the kitchen. It can be used alone in small cubes or sliced on bread, in soufflé or pizza as well as melted in soups or sauces.

Purchase/storage:
There is an enormous variety of Gouda available and you can find it in any discount food store wrapped in foil. It is best to buy it whole so it will not dry out quickly. At home, it should be stored in the refrigerator with cheeses of the same type, wrapped in grease-proof paper enclosed in a plastic case.

Grana Padano

Milk:
🐄 🥛

*Country of
Origin:
Italy*

*Recommended
drink: Red wine,
e.g. Valpolicella*

■ TYPE: Hard cheese

■ ORIGIN AND EXTENT: Grana Padano is produced in the area around the river Po. Venice, Trentino, Piemont, Lombardy and Emilia-Romana.

■ FEATURES: Grana Padano has a cylindrical shape with a slightly convex or almost flat margin. Its diameter is 14 to 18 in, its height is 7 to 10 in and its weight varies between 53 to 88 lbs. Its rind is naturally yellow and the thickness of the rind is 4 to 8 mm. The curd is white to straw-ochre colored, slightly grainy and perforated with tiny holes.

■ PRODUCTION: The cheese is prepared from the milk of cows fed with fresh green feed or hay. The milk comes during two separate milking periods over the course of one day and is then partially skimmed before lactic acid is added. Grana Padano is produced throughout the year. It is matured for up to 2 years at a temperature of 59° to 72°F.

IN THE KITCHEN

AROMA:
Grana Padano has a mild, slightly acidulous and aromatic flavor.

FAT CONTENT:
32% fat in dry mass.

USE:
Grana Padano which has not undergone the maturing process can be used as sliced cheese. The older version is only suitable for grating.

PURCHASE/STORAGE:
Grana Padano is wrapped in foil and is available in discount food stores or in a cheese stand in any larger supermarket. In Germany, it is often offered as Parmesan. But it is cheaper than Parmigiano Reggiano, since it is produced in much larger quantities. Grana Padano can be kept for a long time in whole pieces well packed in the vegetable box of a refrigerator. When grated, it can be stored, tightly closed in a plastic case, for several days in refrigerator.

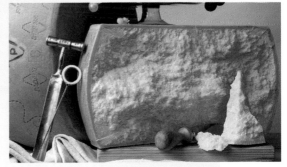

Graucheese

Milk:
🐄 🥛

Country of origin:
Austria

Recommended
drink:
Beer, e.g.
Export

TYPE: Sour milk cheese

ORIGIN AND EXTENT: This farm cheese comes form Tyrol or Styria. The common name for this cheese is "Steirerkas."

FEATURES: Graucheese is offered in the form of slices, wheels or sticks and the weight varies between ½ lb and 7 lbs. Its rind is thin and the curd has narrow cracks and is covered with gray-blue to green-gray mold. The dry curd is yellow and white striped.

PRODUCTION: Graucheese is made of skimmed milk. The milk is soured by means of lactic acid bacteria, which produces a fatless curd. It is poured into forms and matures over a period of 10 days.

HISTORICAL NOTICE: Graucheese was the food of poor people, since there was usually a surplus of skimmed milk left-over when the cream was removed. The soured milk was often left to mature directly besides a stove and so good cheese was created very quickly.

IN THE KITCHEN

AROMA:
Graucheese has a slightly acidulous flavor which grows more pungent during maturation.

FAT CONTENT:
0% fat in dry mass.

USE:
Graucheese is perfect with rye bread and is wonderful when prepared with vinegar.

PURCHASE/STORAGE:
Graucheese can only be found in specialized cheese shops. In Tyrol and Austria, home-made cheese is available in small milk shops. Graucheese should be kept in a plastic box, well-packed for several days and refrigerated, of course.

Greyerzer

Milk:
🐄 🥛

Country of origin:
Switzerland

Recommended drink:
Red wine, e.g. Dôle

■ TYPE: Sliced cheese

■ ORIGIN AND EXTENT: This cheese is also known as Greyerzer. It originates in the county of Greyerzer in the west Swiss canton, Freiburg (Fribourg). Swiss Greyerzer can only be produced in the cantons of Freiburg, Waadt, Neuenburg and Jura and in the districts of Courtelary, La Neuveville, Moutier as well as in several villages on the borders of canton Bern.

■ FEATURES: The round wheels of Greyerzer are 4 to 5 in high with 23 to 26 in diameters. The weight of one wheel ranges from 77 to 88 lbs. The brown rind is grainy and greasy. The edge of the cheese is slightly convex. The consistency of the dough is rather firm, not crumbly. The cheese is penetrated by holes with diameters of 4 to 5 mm.

■ PRODUCTION: Greyerzer cheese is produced from the raw milk of cows fed grass during the summer and hay in the winter. The raw milk must be processed within 18 hours after milking. The milk is heated in open copper kettles. The volume of kettle must not exceed 1,745 gallons. Rennet is added to the milk and the curd is crushed and heated again under stirring. Then the cheese mass is put into forms and is pressed at least for 16 hours. The pressure is gradually increased. Firm pressure is necessary to drain the whey and produce firm texture. As the cheese is formed, it is salted. The cheese is kept at a temperature between 54° to 64°F and humidity above 90% on stands made from spruce wood. During the first 8 to 12 days, the body of the cheese is ground and turned over daily. The cheese matures for period of 5 to 12 months.

■■■ HISTORIC NOTE: The production of the cheese in this region was established by charter in the year 1155. The farmers were allowed to produce cheese. The material, such as kettles, harps and molds, were donated by clergy. Further documents give evidence that the cheese market existed in the town of Freiburg since 1249. In the 14th century, the cheese was known outside Switzerland and during the 30 years of war, this cheese was an important source of food. Since this

time, there have been attempts to protect the production of the cheese. Formerly, a large "G" on the cheese loaves marked Greyerzer cheese. At an agricultural exhibition in Paris, two dairies were awarded high prizes for their cheeses, increasing demand for this cheese considerably. Following this, it was exported to English and Dutch colonies. Today, the cheese is protected by an AOC–impression and is exported far from the Swiss border.

Cheese fondue

▬ INGREDIENTS: 1 lb Greyerzer and Emmentaler •
1 clove of garlic • 1 – 2 cups white wine • 1 teaspoon lemon
juice • 1–2 liqueur glasses cherry brandy • 4 teaspoons starch •
fresh pepper • baguette or rye bread

▬ PREPARATION: Rub the fondue pot with the garlic, grate
the cheese and heat while stirring together with wine and
lemon juice until all of the cheese has melted. Add the starch
dissolved in the cherry brandy and boil briefly. Add the pepper. Cut the bread into small cubes. Put the fondue pot on the
cooking range. Occasionally stir the fondue to prevent the
cheese from settling onto the bottom.

IN THE KITCHEN

AROMA:
Greyerzer has a mellow, slightly salty flavor.

FAT CONTENT:
49% fat in dry mass.

USE:
Because of its excellent melting qualities, Greyerzer is used in soufflés, sauces and cheese fondue. It is consumed with bread and vegetables.

PURCHASE/STORAGE:
You can find Greyerzer cheese in a cheese shop or grocery store. It can be refrigerated whole at home, alone or with cheeses of the same type, wrapped in grease-proof paper and in perforated aluminum foil.

HAVE YOU TRIED...?

FILLED BRIOCHES: **Prepare Béchamel sauce, mix with cubes of cooked ham, grated Greyerzer cheese and egg yolk. Add whipped egg whites. Cut small brioches into slices, hollow them and fill them with cheese mixture. Bake in the oven at a medium temperature.**

Havarti

■ TYPE: sliced cheese

■ ORIGIN AND EXTENT: Like Esrom, Havarti originates on Seeland, an island off the Danish coast.

■ FEATURES: Havarti is molded into rectangular or round shapes. Its weight ranges between 4 and 10 lbs. The curd of the cheese is light yellow and full of small round holes. The thin, natural rind is washed. Sometimes, the cheese is covered with a layer of red wax.

■ PRODUCTION: To produce Havarti, pasteurized cow's milk is soured and then broken into small pieces, put into the forms and pressed slightly. After adding salt, the cheese matures for at least 1 month. Spices or herbs can be added. The cheese is sold in various stages of maturity.

■ HISTORICAL NOTICE: Havarti obtained its name from a Danish farm house, "Havartigaarden," which belonged to Hanne Nielson. One hundred years ago, Nielson traveled through Europe learning about cheese production and later founded her own dairy in Denmark.

IN THE KITCHEN

AROMA:
The more mature Havarti has a more piquant flavor.

FAT CONTENT:
30% fat in dry mass.

USE:
Havarti is typically a sandwich cheese. It is consumed with tomatoes and pickles. Havarti cheese with greater fat content can be used for baking.

PURCHASE/STORAGE:
Havarti can be found in cheese shops. It should be refrigerated whole, wrapped in greaseproof paper and foil.

Herrgårdost

Milk:
🐄 🥛

Country of origin:
Sweden

Recommended drink:
White wine,
e.g. Silvaner

■ TYPE: Sliced cheese

■ ORIGIN AND EXTENT: This cheese comes from Sweden and its name is translated into English as "lord's cheese." It can be assumed that this cheese was traditionally produced in the larger yards of middle and southern Sweden.

■ FEATURES: The size and shape of Herrgårdost is similar to a cartwheel. Its weight is between 26 and 44 lbs. The cheese has a firm consistency and a pale yellow color, and the holes inside are the size of peas.

■ PRODUCTION: Herrgårdost is produced from pasteurized cow's milk. The milk is soured by rennet, cut up, heated while stirring and pressed into forms. The cheese is adequate after three months, but it must mature longer for a firmer texture and stronger flavor.

■ SIMILAR CHEESES: *Greve* differs only slightly from Herrgårdost. It has the same cartwheel shape, but it is smaller. It matures in 10 months and its aroma is mild.

IN THE KITCHEN

AROMA:
Herrgårdost is mild with a slightly nutty flavor.

FAT CONTENT:
28% fat in dry mass.

USE:
In Sweden, Herrgårdost is traditionally consumed with bread for lunch. Because of its greater fat content, it is suitable for baking.

PURCHASE/STORAGE:
Herrgårdost can be found in cheese shops. It should be stored whole in the vegetable box of a refrigerator, wrapped in grease-proof paper and perforated foil.

Herve

Milk:

Country of
origin:
Belgium

Recommended
drink: Bier,
e.g. Starkbier

■ TYPE: Soft cheese

■ ORIGIN AND EXTENT: Herve comes from the province of Liège in Belgium.

■ FEATURES: Herve has a rectangular shape and can be found in four weights: 2, 3½, 7, 14 oz. The curd is ivory-colored and contains very few holes. The rind is orange-yellow and slightly moist.

■ PRODUCTION: Herve is produced from pasteurized cow's milk. The milk is heated and treated with rennet. After 1 to 1½ hours, the curd is cut into pieces the size of hazelnuts. The curd is removed from the whey, formed into squares and slightly pressed. The cheese is painted red and matures in wet cellar rooms for 5 to 6 weeks. During its maturation period, the cheese is washed with salt brine several times per week in order to fully develop the aroma of the cheese. Herve, known as "extra piquant," matures at least 2 months to render its flavor and scent more pungent.

IN THE KITCHEN

AROMA:
Herve has a very intense, piquant and spicy flavor and smell.

FAT CONTENT:
45% fat in dry mass.

USE:
This cheese is served alone with beer or at the end of the meal. It is delicious spread on toast. This cheese is only for cheese fans since most people find its smell rather offensive.

PURCHASE/STORAGE:
Herve can be found in cheese shops. Wrapped in grease-proof paper and tightly closed in its case, it keeps well in a refrigerator.

Ibérico

Milk:

Country of origin:
Spain

Recommended
drink:
Red wine,
e.g. Rioja

■ TYPE: Semi-hard, sliced cheese

■ ORIGIN AND EXTENT: Ibérico is industrially produced in the central plateau of the Iberian Peninsula. The origin is not protected and therefore it is produced freely throughout Spain.

■ FEATURES: Ibérico is a cylindrical cheese with a diameter of 8 in and a height of 6 in. Its weight varies between 7 and 9 lb. The cheese is covered with a layer of paraffin or plastic to prevent it from drying. The color of the rind shows the stage of its maturity. The white or light yellow rind always denotes the young cheese, which has been maturing for 25 to 30 days. The black rind denotes the half-mature, which is 50 to 60 days old. 3 months old cheese has brown rind and the fully mature cheese, after 6 months, has dark brown rind.

■ PRODUCTION: Ibérico is the best known Spanish mixed cheese. It is produced from pasteurized cow, goat and sheep's milk, each of which must be present in the cheese in proportions of 25 to 40%. The milk mixture is soured by rennet and then the cheese is formed and salted. It matures for at least 25 days.

IN THE KITCHEN

AROMA:
Young and half-mature cheese has a fresh, mildly spicy aroma. The more mature the cheese, the more powerful and piquant the flavor.

FAT CONTENT:
45% fat in dry mass.

USE:
Ibérico is the most commonly used cheese in Spain. It is used for baking and to improve the flavor of hot dishes. It is also served alone with wine and bread.

PURCHASE/STORAGE:
Ibérico can be found in cheese shops or in Spanish specialty shops. It can be stored, well packed, in the vegetable box of a refrigerator.

Ibores

▬ TYPE: Semi-hard, sliced cheese

▬ ORIGIN AND EXTENT: The home of Ibores is Extremadura, a region in southwestern Spain. It is a plateau surrounded by steep mountains with many pastures and oak trees.

▬ FEATURES: Ibores has a cylindrical shape and its weight ranges from 1 to 3 lbs. The cheese has a natural rind, into which greased paprika powder or olive oil is added during the maturation period, coloring the cheese either red or ochre.

▬ PRODUCTION: Ibores is produced from the raw milk of three breeds of goats: Serrana, Verata and Retinta. The souring is achieved by means of natural rennet. When it reaches middle age, the cheese mass is half-firm. The rind is then treated with olive oil or with smoked paprika powder from La Vera. The cheese must mature at least two months before it is sold.

▬ HISTORICAL NOTE: In the almost untouched chains of mountains in Villuercas and Ibor, the shepherds live a traditional, nomadic life. The milk and meat of their goats serves as the only supply of food for the shepherds and their families.

IN THE KITCHEN

AROMA:
Ibores has a slightly buttery and unobtrusive aroma typical of goat's milk.

FAT CONTENT:
45% fat in dry mass.

USE:
Ibores is commonly consumed with bread. But it can be grated to improve the flavor of soufflé, fish dishes, sauces and soups.

PURCHASE/STORAGE:
Ibores can be found in cheese shops or in Spanish specialty shops. It can be stored, well packed, in the vegetable box of a refrigerator.

DID YOU KNOW THAT...?

Homemade cheese was first sold in markets, particularly in Trujillo, to so-called Afinadores who let the cheese mature longer and later sold it again. In last 15 years, migratory shepherds settled and produced the cheese in small dairies.

Idiazábal

Milk:
🧀 ▯

Country of origin:
Spain

Recommended drink:
Red wine,
e.g. Rioja

TYPE: Hard cheese

ORIGIN AND EXTENT: Idiazábal comes from the Basque country and takes its name from a Basque village. Idiazábal is produced throughout the Basque Territory and in the northwestern part of Navarra.

FEATURES: Idiazábal has a cylindrical shape and its weight ranges between 2 and 7 lbs. The cheese mass is firm, almost crumbly, and has an ivory color. If the rind is light yellow, then the cheese is not smoked. If the rind is red-orange to brown, then it is the smoked variant.

PRODUCTION: Idiazábal is produced from the milk of the Latxa and Carranzana sheep. The goat's milk is soured by means of natural rennet. The curd is minced, then pressed and put into a traditional mold. After salting, it matures for 2 to 5 months. These stages can be followed by smoking the cheese in a fire of beech, hawthorn or cherry wood.

IN THE KITCHEN

AROMA:

Idiazábal has a slightly piquant and expressive sheep flavor. The non-smoked variant has a weak aroma of hay.

FAT CONTENT:

45% fat in dry mass.

USE:

Idiazábal is consumed raw for brunch and is also used in grated form for cooking, baking and to improve the flavor of dishes.

PURCHASE/STORAGE:

Idiazábal can be found in cheese shops or in Spanish specialty shops. The cheese should be stored, well packed, in the vegetable box of a refrigerator.

DID YOU KNOW THAT....?

At one time, the shepherds returned to the valley every fall with their herds. During the summer months, they produced Idiazábal in the chalets. They smoked the cheese above the open fire to improve its durability and sold it in cattle markets in the valley during the winter.

Jarlsberg

Milk:
🐄 🥛

Country of origin:
Norway

Recommended
drink:
White wine,
e.g. Riesling

TYPE: Sliced cheese

ORIGIN AND EXTENT: This cheese comes from the region of Jarlsberg in southern Norway. It is probably the oldest sliced cheese in Norway and takes its name from an old Viking seat in Oslofjord. Today, this cheese is exported mainly to the United States, Australia, New Zealand and Japan and throughout the European Union. Consumption of Jarlsberg cheese abroad is four times greater than in Norway.

FEATURES: Jarlsberg is a round cheese with a diameter of about 12 in, a height of 4 in and a weight of about 22 lb. The curd is golden-yellow with hazelnut-sized holes. Due to its large holes, in Norway it is called "Emmentaler of Fjords."

PRODUCTION: In summer, the cows pasture on lush and slightly salty meadows above the fjords. The milk is soured with rennet, and the curd is then cut up, heated and pressed into molds for two days. Then the cheese is washed in salt brine. It matures for at least 100 days, but also spends up to 10 months in cool cellars. During this time, it is regularly washed and brushed.

IN THE KITCHEN

AROMA:
Jarlsberg has a mild and nutty flavor.

FAT CONTENT:
45% fat in dry mass.

USE:
Jarlsberg is well suited for consumption with bread. Together with other Norwegian specialties such as pickled herrings or salmon, it is commonly consumed for breakfast. Slices of Jarlsberg are also served after a traditional hot supper. It is often used for baking.

PURCHASE/STORAGE:
Jarlsberg can be found closed in cooled bags in cheese shops, sometimes in large super-markets or on cheese stands. It can be stored whole, wrapped in grease-proof paper and aluminum foil, in the vegetable box of a refrigerator.

Kefalotiri

Milk:

Country of origin:
Greece

Recommended
drink:
White wine,
e.g. Mandilari

TYPE: sliced cheese

ORIGIN AND EXTENT: Kefalotiri is produced throughout Greece and it is named after the region of its origin.

FEATURES: The name is derived from the Greek word "Kefalo," meaning a Greek hat which has a similar shape. The cheese weighs about 22 lb and its height is about 10 in. The diameter is approximately 20 in.

PRODUCTION: Kefalotiri is produced from raw goat or sheep's milk. The soured milk is pressed into forms, salted and pressed again. The cheese matures for 2 to 3 months in cool and wet cellars.

ANOTHER SORT: Kasseri is young Kafalotiri. Its consistency is more elastic as it is poured into hot water during the production process. This cheese is sold as a disk or block.

IN THE KITCHEN

AROMA:
Kefalotiri has a slightly salty, mildly acidulous flavor.

FAT CONTENT:
45% fat in dry mass.

USE:
Kefalotiri is used in the preparation of Mossaka and other hot Greek dishes.

PURCHASE AND STORAGE:
Kefalotiri can be bought in Greek or Turkish food shops. It can be kept whole for several days in the vegetable box of a refrigerator, wrapped in grease-proof paper and foil.

Laguiole

Milk:
🐄 🥛

Country of
Origin:
France

Recommended
drink:
Red wine, e.g.
fruity Beaujolais

TYPE: sliced cheese

ORIGIN AND EXTENT: Laguiole comes originally from Aubrac, a basalt plateau approximately 1 mile high. As an AOC cheese, it may only be produced in the departments of Aveyron, Cantal and LozÈre of southern Auvergne.

FEATURES: Laguiole has a cylindrical shape. Its diameter and height are 16 in and it weighs between 99 to 106 lbs. The consistency of the cheese is supple and elastic. The older the cheese, the more crumbly it is.

PRODUCTION: According to tradition, Laguiole is produced in chalets or dairies. When formed, the curd matures under the press. Then it is broken again into small pieces, the dough is salted and filled into special molds lined with cloth. After the new pressing, the cheese matures 4 to 9 months in cellars.

HISTORICAL NOTE: The cheese production in this region has a long tradition. Pliny talks about it in his work. Laguiole was first mentioned in the 4th century.

IN THE KITCHEN

AROMA:
Laguiole is slightly acidulous with a very piquant flavor.

FAT CONTENT:
45% fat in dry mass.

USE:
This cheese can be consumed with bread. As a grated cheese, it is good for baking and gratinated dishes.

PURCHASE AND STORAGE:
Laguiole can be found only in specialized shops. It can be recognized by the name engraved in the rind. The cheese should be stored whole wrapped in the grease-proof paper and perforated aluminum foil in the vegetable box of a refrigerator.

HAVE YOU TRIED...?

To make your potato purée more delicate, add butter, 1 minced love garlic, a little cooked bacon and a small cup of cream at a mild temperature. Then add 14 oz grated Laguiole and beat the purée vigorously with a spoon. Add pepper, salt and serve with homemade bread and green salad.

Langres

Milk:
🐄 🥛

Country of origin:
France

Recommended
drink:
Strong red wine
from Burgundy,
or Marc de
Champagne

■ TYPE: Sliced cheese with a washed rind

■ ORIGIN AND EXTENT: The home of Langres lies on the border of Champagne, Burgundy and Lothringen. The cheese is produced in the departments of Côte d'Or, Haute-Marne and Vogese. The name comes from the name of the plateau situated in this region.

■ FEATURES: Langres has a washed rind. Thus it is always slightly moist and brightly colored, (depending on the stage of its maturity,) ranging from light yellow to brown. The cheese is ivory-colored and becomes creamier during the maturation process. There is a conspicuous depression on the upper side of the cheese. Langres is produced in two sizes: the larger is cylindrical with a height of 2 to 8 in, a diameter of 6 to 8 in and it weighs at least 1½ lb. The smaller one only reaches a height of 2 to 2½ in, a diameter of 3 to 3½ in and a weight of 5 lb.

■ PRODUCTION: This cheese is produced exclusively from cow's milk. The curd is put into molds without previous stirring or salting. The curd is then left to drain in the molds for 24 hours before being salted and dried. During its maturation the cheese creates its red culture and, until the end of its maturation, Marc de Bourgogne or champagne is poured into

the depression on the upper side and absorbed into the cheese. The process is repeated several times and the depression becomes larger and larger. The small variant of Langres matures in at least 15 days, the larger variant finishes the maturation process in no less then 21 days.

■■■ HISTORICAL NOTE: This cheese was praised in an 18th century song. Formerly Langres was prepared from still-warm milk after milking. The milk was poured into containers made from burnt clay. After forming, the cheese was dried and matured on the oat straw.

Langres in puff pastry

■ INGREDIENTS: 1 lb mushrooms • ½-1 cup créme fraiche • 5 oz Langres • salt and pepper • 3½ tablespoons butter • 1 teaspoon flour • 1 packet puff pastry (frozen) • 1 egg

■ PREPARATION: Defrost the puff pastry and cut the pieces of the pastry into 4x4 in. Beat the egg, use it to grease the pastry pieces and then bake them in the oven at 428°F. Slit the baked pieces of pastry. Pare the mushrooms and mix them in the pan with the créme fraiche and let boil 3 to 4 min. Mix the butter and flour and add to the mushrooms. Divide the mushroom mixture into two parts. Put a tablespoons of mushrooms into each of the baked pieces of pastry, cover with slices of cheese, add another piece and bake all together for 5 min. at 248°F. Then put all on a warm plate and pour on the remaining mushroom mixture. The dish is served moderately hot.

IN THE KITCHEN

AROMA:
Langres has a strong and spicy flavor and intensive smell.

FAT CONTENT:
50% fat in dry mass.

USE:
Langres, as well as Roquefort, is essential to any well-planned cheese plate. The classic combination consists of Langres, baked plums and almonds. In spite of its intense smell, it is suitable for hot cuisine.

PURCHASE/STORAGE:
Langres can only be found in special shops. When keeping overnight, wrap in grease-proof paper in a tightly closed case in refrigerator vegetable box. However, it is best to consume it immediately after purchase.

HAVE YOU TRIED…?
Pour a little Marc de Champagne into the depression in the cheese, allow the cheese time to absorb it and then enjoy with bacon bread.

Leerdammer

Milk:

🐄 🥛

Country of origin: Netherlands

Recommended drink: Beer, e.g. Export

■ TYPE: sliced cheese

■ ORIGIN AND EXTENT: In the Netherlands, the cheese is known as Maasdammer. It is produced throughout the Netherlands.

■ FEATURES: At the first sight, this cheese could be mistaken for Emmentaler. The round, slightly convex cheese with its large holes resembles Swiss cheese, but the volume is much smaller. Its weight ranges between 13 to 31 lb. The cheese has a thin, yellow rind covered by wax.

■ PRODUCTION: Leerdammer is a cheese with a young history. Legend has it that a dairy master tried to create a cheese as supple as Gouda and with a nutty aroma similar to Emmentaler. The result of this was Leerdammer. Leerdammer is produced from pasteurized cow's milk and matures for 5 weeks. It has a shorter maturation period than either Gouda or Emmentaler.

> HAVE YOU TRIED ...?
> **Leerdammer is very delicious on toast with grape jelly or raspberry jam.**

IN THE KITCHEN

AROMA:
Leerdammer is a fresh, mild, slightly nutty cheese.

FAT CONTENT:
45% fat in dry mass.

USE:
Leerdammer is typically used for spreading on bread. Grapes, tomatoes and pickles go with it very well.

PURCHASE/STORAGE:
Leerdammer can be found in supermarkets packed in foil as well as on any cheese stand. It is best to buy it whole. For storage at home, store it alone or with cheeses of the same type, wrapped in grease-proof paper in the plastic case in a refrigerator.

Limburger

Milk:
🐄 🥛

Country of origin:
Germany

Recommended
drink: Red wine,
e.g. Dornfelder

■ TYPE: soft cheese

■ ORIGIN AND EXTENT: Limburger originated in Belgium and was named after the province of Limbourg. In the mid-19th century Belgian workers brought the cheese to Allgäu. Because of its shape and size, Limburger is commonly called "brick cheese."

■ FEATURES: Limburger is sold as a rod with a weight of 7 oz to 2 lbs. The rind is covered with sticky, red-brown grease. The light yellow cheese is dull and soft with a firm consistency. When mature, Limburger is elastic and soft, but not liquid. It has small, irregular holes.

■ PRODUCTION: During the production of Limburger, the cow's milk is soured by rennet, then roughly cut up and poured into perforated molds. When the whey drains, the cheese is removed from the mold and poured for short time into brine. Then it matures for 3 to 4 weeks, during which it is regularly washed with brine and turned over. Thus, the creation of red grease is stimulated.

In the kitchen

AROMA:
Limburger has a spicy, piquant flavor and a distinctive scent.

FAT CONTENT:
20% fat in dry mass.

USE:
Limburger is a favorite cheese in Germany and is consumed with rye caraway bread and slices of red onion. Because of its greater fat content, Limburger can be used for baking in potato or vegetable dishes.

PURCHASE/STORAGE:
Limburger, or Romadur, can be found on any large cheese stand. Well-packed in a box, it can be stored for several days in a refrigerator.

DID YOU KNOW THAT…?

Romadur, a relation of Limburger, also originated in Belgium. Formerly, it was the fattier and more piquant cousin of Limburger, but today, it differs in size and flavor. Loaves of Romadur weigh between 3 and 3½ oz, but at the time of its maturity, it is the same size as Limburger. The aroma of Romadur is also more piquant.

Livarot

Milk:
🐄 🥛

Country of origin:
Frankreich

Recommended
drink:
Apfelwein, z. B.
Cidre aus der
Normandie

■ TYPE: Soft cheese with washed rind

■ ORIGIN AND EXTENT: This cheese originated in a very small area of Pays d'Auge in Normandy. Now this cheese has the AOC-impression, but can be produced only in the departments of Calvados and Orne.

■ FEATURES: Livarot has a washed, reddish rind. Along the edge, we can find five stripes, formerly made with lines of willow wood and now made with paper. Due to these stripes, the cheese is commonly known as "Colonel." The cheese is elastic and cream-colored. It is cylindrical with a height of about 2 in. It is available in four different diameters: 5 in, 4 in, 3½ and 3 in. Its weight ranges between ½ to 1 lb.

■ PRODUCTION: The cow's milk is soured by rennet. The curd is cut up and kneaded. After the whey is drawn, the cheese is formed, salted and turned over many times. Livarot is then stored at least one month in the cellar where it matures. During this period, the cheese is washed and turned over three times per week. Five strips of paper are bound around the margin. These strips enable the cheese to keep its cylindrical shape during the maturation period.

IN THE KITCHEN

AROMA:
Livarot has an aromatic smell and its flavor is acrid, slightly acidulous and spicy.

FAT CONTENT:
40% fat in dry mass.

USE:
Livarot appears at the end of a meal, but it is also an essential part of a cheese plate. It is rarely used in hot cuisine.

PURCHASE/STORAGE:
The best Livarot can be found in specialized shops from the fall until the end of spring. It is sold unpacked or in a special wooden box. If stored overnight, it should be wrapped whole in grease-proof paper and placed in a tightly closed case in the vegetable box of a refrigerator. Ideally it should be consumed immediately after purchase.

DID YOU KNOW THAT…?

In 1877, 4.5 million Livarot cheeses matured in about 200 cheese cellars. In that time, this cheese was produced in greater quantities than any other cheese. It was the most consumed cheese in Normandy, where it was referred to as the "meat of poor people."

Mahón-Menorca

Milk:
🐄 🥛

Country of origin:
Spain

Recommended
drink:
White wine
e.g. Cava

■ TYPE: Semi-hard, sliced cheese

■ ORIGIN AND EXTENT: The home of Mahón is Minorca, one of the Balearic Islands and the cheese was named after the capital of the island.

■ FEATURES: Mahón has a rectangular shape with rounded edges. The rind is pale or orange yellow and when traditionally produced dark lines form, due to greasing by olive oil, on its surface. The cheese is ivory-colored and less elastic. Its weight ranges between 2 and 9 lbs.

■ PRODUCTION: Mahón is made from pasteurized cow's milk. The milk comes from following breeds of cattle: Mahonesa, Frisona and Pardo-alpina. The milk is heated up to 91°F and soured by rennet, before being cut up, mixed, formed and put into brine. Then it matures in special cellars and is turned over regularly. The minimum time for maturity is 3 weeks.

■ HISTORICAL NOTE: The first written evidence of the production of cheese in the island of Minorca is from the 5th century. Until the English occupation, cheese was produced from sheep's milk.

■ VARIANTS: *Mahón.* The young cheese, which matures only 3 to 9 weeks, is white with a thin rind and a milky aroma.

Mahón semicurado, the half-mature cheese, is 2 months old. Its rind is orange and its curd is firm with small holes. Its flavor is strong, resembling butter and roasted nuts.

Mahón curado undergoes 6 months of maturation. Its aroma is piquant, its consistency firm and slightly crumbly.

Mahón anejo matures at least 10 months and its aroma is more pronounced. The curd is hard and friable.

Mahón with parsley

■ INGREDIENTS: 7 oz Mahón • 7 table-spoons flour • 2 eggs • 1 tablespoon milk • 1 bunch of parsley • olive oil • salt

■ PREPARATION: Cut the cheese into rectangular pieces about 1 in thick and sprinkle with flour. Wash the parsley, dry and cut finely. Beat the eggs with the milk and add the pieces of the cheese to the mixture. Then sprinkle more flour. Heat the olive oil in the frying pan and fry the cheese until brown. Drain, sprinkle with the minced parsley and serve warm.

HAVE YOU TRIED...?

Cut the baguette in slices, heat a little butter in the pan together with thin slices of Mahón, transfer all onto a baking sheet and put under the grill for 5 to 7 minutes until the cheese starts to melt. This complements salad with sherry vinegar dressing.

IN THE KITCHEN

AROMA:

Light taste reminiscent of the sea: acidulous and salty flavor.

FAT CONTANT

38% fat in dry mass.

USE:

The young Mahón is consumed with bread. The older the cheese, the tastier it is in soufflés, meat dishes, sauces and soups as well as in the Spanish dish, tapas.

PURCHASE/STORAGE:

Mahón can be found in cheese shops or in Spanish specialty shops. It is available throughout the year. It should be stored, securely packed, in the vegetable box of a refrigerator.

Mainzer Cheese

Milk:
🐄 🥛

Country of origin:
Germany

Recommended
drink:
Apple wine

■ TYPE: Soured milk cheese

■ ORIGIN AND EXTENT: Like Harz cheese produced at the foot of the Harz Mountains and Olomouc cheese from Olomouc, Mainzer was originally produced in Mainz. Since the end of the 19th century, Mainz, Olomouc and Harz have been known for their sour milk cheese industries.

■ FEATURES: The common feature of these cheeses is their weight of 1 to 7 oz. The curd is yellow and firm to supple. The shape is mostly rounded, the rind is thin and it is covered with white mold of Mamembert, or with red grease.

■ PRODUCTION: The milk used for this cheese is pasteurized cow's milk. The milk is lightly heated and lactic acid bacteria added. The soured milk is removed from the whey and molded. Formerly, the cheeses were put into baskets to enable the whey to drain and were then molded manually.

IN THE KITCHEN

AROMA:
Sour milk cheese has a mildly piquant flavor and its aroma is unique and slightly acidulous. Caraway is often added. When the cheese is well matured, its smell is very pronounced and not everyone will appreciate it.

FAT CONTENT:
0.5% absolute fat.

USE:
All cheeses of this kind are well suited for rye bread. Creative cooks prefer to hide this cheese in salad. This cheese is not designed for eating hot. "Handkäse mit Musik" is a specialty from Frankfurt. The cheese is pickled in a mixture of vinegar, oil, onion salt and pepper.

PURCHASE/STORAGE:
Sour milk cheese can be found in any larger cheese stand as well as also packed and cold in supermarkets. It can be kept in a refrigerator for several days tightly closed in a plastic case.

DO YOU KNOW THAT...?
Sour milk cheese is a cheese tradition as old as raising of cattle in the northern Alps. It is produced from surplus milk and represents an opportunity to utilize spoiled milk.

Majorero

Milk:

Country of origin:
Spain

Recommended
drink:
Red wine e.g.
Rioja

▬ TYPE: Sliced cheese

▬ ORIGIN AND EXTENT: The Canary Islands are home to Majorero. It is produced in Fuerteventura.

▬ FEATURES: The cylindrical loaves of Majorero have a diameter ranging from 6 to 14 in and a weight between 2 and 13 lbs. The natural rind is treated either with Gofio, rough corn flour, or paprika powder and therefore the color is either floury white or red. A pattern of palm-tree leaves is traditionally engraved on the upper and lower sides of the mature cheese. These leaves were used in the formation of the cheese.

▬ PRODUCTION: Majorero is made from the pasteurized milk of Majorera goats. These animals are excellently acclimated to the conditions prevailing on the island and give extra creamy milk. The milk is soured by addition of enzymes. The sour is then pressed and matures for various time periods.

▬ HISTORICAL NOTE: The name of the cheese originates from the Middle Ages. The adjective "majorero" has been derived from the name of the island, Fuerteventura "Maxorata."

▬ VARIANTS: *Majorero* tierno is not mature. It is a curd cheese, prepared in the same way from goat's milk and it is consumed without being matured.

Majorero semicurado is half-mature at 3 months old and its aroma is very pronounced.

Majorero curado matures for 4 months and has a roasted aroma.

Bread filled with cheese

▬ INGREDIENTS: 1 medium loaf white bread • 7 oz Majorero • 3 tablespoons cracked nuts

▬ PREPARATION: If possible, choose a tall loaf of white bread and cut off the top slice to be used as a lid. Remove the soft part from the loaf. Then fill the hollow with chopped nuts and place the cheese on them. Fill the remaining space in the hollow with more chopped nuts and cover it with the bread slice. Let the oven preheat to 392°F and heat the bread about 15 minutes till the cheese is melted. When the loaf of bread is too large, it is necessary to use more cheese and to heat it only 10 minutes in the oven. Serve immediately. The large bread is enough for 8 people. Everyone simply breaks off a piece of bread crust and scoops out some of the mixture from the inside.

It is also possible to fill small sandwiches with the same mixture. Strong red wine is a suitable drink for this dish.

IN THE KITCHEN

AROMA:
Majorero has a slightly piquant and acidulous flavor. The more mature the cheese, the more balanced and pronounced the flavor of the goat's milk. Older cheeses have sharper flavor as a rule.

FAT CONTENT:
55% fat in dry mass.

USE:
Majorero is consumed with salad or on bread. The older the cheese, the better it is in soufflés, fish dishes, soups and sauces.

PURCHASE /STORAGE:
Majorero can be found in cheese shops or in Spanish specialty shops. Or, better yet, travel to the island of Fuerteventura. Store carefully wrapped mature cheese in the vegetable box of a refrigerator.

Manchego

Milk:
🧀 🥛

Country of origin:
Spain

Reccommanded
drink:
Dessert wine,
e.g. Sherry fino

■ TYPE: Hard cheese

■ ORIGIN AND EXTENT: Manchego is the most well-known Spanish cheese and it is exported throughout the world. It originates in the La Mancha region, a large plateau in central Spain with the special climatic conditions characteristic of the landscape.

■ FEATURES: Manchego has a cylindrical shape with a diameter of 10 in and a height of 3 in. Its weight ranges from 5½ to 7 lbs. The rind has a conspicuous zigzag pattern and may be yellow or black, depending on the production. The use of olive oil makes the rind black. The curd is compact and firm, but not very elastic. The ivory-colored mass only has a few holes.

■ PRODUCTION: Manchego is produced from pasteurized sheep's milk. The milk comes exclusively from the very robust but small sheep of Manchego. The milk sours at a temperature of 82° to 90° F with natural rennet. The sour is then stirred, the whey is left to drain and then the cheese mass is pressed. Then the curd is poured into cylindrical forms and pressed again. The cheese is subsequently pickled in the brine for 24 hours. A salted cheese undergoes maturation at a temperature of 46°

to 54°F and a relative humidity of 80 to 85%. Maturation lasts at least 2 months.

■■■ HISTORICAL NOTE: Miguel de Cervantes mentioned Manchego in his famous novel "Don Quixote," in which he described the cheese as "harder then if made from sand and lime."

■■■ VARIANTS: *Manchego curado* matures at least 2 months and is greasier than that of older cheese.
Manchego vieja matures at least 9 to 12 months in moist cellars and its rind is regularly washed.

Manchego con aceite: The description "con aceite" means that Manchego is pickled in olive oil, which can be recognized by the dark rind.

Manchego artesano: The description "artesano" indicates that the cheese was made from raw milk.

Zamorano: comes from the region Castilien-León which belongs to the province of Zamora. It is produced similarly to Manchego. The milk is from sheep breeds, Churra and Castellana. The cheese must mature at least 100 days and its aroma is distinctly spicy.

HAVE YOU TRIED...?

QUESO FRITO: Remove the rind from 1 lb Manchego and cut it into 1 in cubes. Prepare three bowls. In the first, beat 2 eggs with 2 teaspoons of cream; in the second, mix a little flour with 3½ tablespoons of almonds; in the third bowl, place only flour. The pieces of cheese are firstly floured, then submerged in the egg mixture and finally dipped in the flour and almond mixture. Then the pieces of cheese are fried in olive oil until golden brown. Drain and serve warm.

IN THE KITCHEN

AROMA:
Manchego has a strong, spicy flavor. The older the cheese, the more piquant the flavor.

FAT CONTENT:
55% fat in dry mass.

USE:
Manchego is used in the preparation of tapas. It is consumed either raw or fried in oil. The older the cheese, the better it is for grating. It can be used to mildly flavor soufflés, meat dishes, soups and sauces.

PURCHASE/STORAGE:
Manchego can be found in cheese shops, shops with Spanish specialties and also on the cheese stands of larger supermarkets. This cheese is available throughout the whole year. It should be stored, well packed, in the vegetable box of the refrigerator.

Maroilles

Milk:

Country of origin:
France

Recommended
drink:
Beer or Cider

▬ TYPE: soft cheese with washed rind

▬ ORIGIN AND EXTENT: The home of Maroilles is in northern France on the Belgian border. Maroilles cheese bearing the AOC impression comes from Picardy, the northern part of Nord and from the northern part of Aisne.

▬ FEATURES: Maroilles has a washed, orange yellow rind. The square shape resembles a tile. The length of each edge is 5 in and the width is 2 in. The weight is about 2 lbs. There are also three other variants with the following names and weights: "Sorbais" with a weight of 1 lb, "Mignon," weighing slightly less than 1 lb and the smallest one, "Quart."

▬ PRODUCTION: The cow's milk is soured with rennet, then the whey is drained and the cheese is molded and washed. After molding, it is stored in a dry ventilated room where the cover of mold is created over 8 to 10 days. The mold is removed by brushing and washing. Then the cheese matures for 3 to 5 weeks in cellars. Only in the cellars of Thiérache do the special surface film and distinctive aroma develop.

▬ HISTORICAL NOTE: The cheese has a 1,000 year long tradition and was probably invented by monks. It was the

favorite cheese of famous French kings, notably Charles VI and Francois I.

■ Related cheese: *Baguette Laonnaise* is produced similarly to Maroilles. The cheese is made into 1 lb blocks and the soft cheese is surrounded by red flora.

Rollet or Rollet Coeur is cylindrical or heart-shaped. It comes from Picardy and is also soft with a margin of red grease prepared using a similar method. Louis XIV, the Sun King, liked it very much.

Dauphin or Dauphine. This variant comes from Hainaut and has an extremely sharp smell. The cheese was named after the son and prince royal of Louis XIV. The formed Maroilles is minced and mixed with tarragon and pepper, manually formed and then matured for 2 to 3 months.

Quiche

▬ INGREDIENTS: 1 cup flour • 4 eggs • salt • 5 oz butter • 5 oz streaky bacon • 1 cup cream • pepper • 9 oz Maroilles

▬ PREPARATION: Knead together flour, 1 egg, salt and butter, leave covered in a cool place for 20 minutes. In the meantime, cut the bacon into slices. Beat the cream, remaining eggs, salt and pepper together. Roll out the dough on a pastry board, place in a greased pie dish (diameter 11 in) and press the margin to the mold using a fork. Put the bacon on the dough and pour cream mixture over it. Bake the qiuche in a preheated oven at 392°F for 15 minutes. Then add the cheese to the surface of the quiche.

IN THE KITCHEN

AROMA:
Maroilles has an expressive, strong smell, which is why it obtained the attribute "vieux puant," or "old stinker." The older the cheese, the more spicy and strong its flavor.

FAT CONTENT:
45% fat in dry mass.

USE:
Maroilles can be consumed in three stages: not yet mature, or "white," half-mature, or "blond," and fully mature, "old." Many regional dishes use this cheese. It is often served for dessert at the end of a meal.

PURCHASE/STORAGE:
The best Maroilles can be found in specialty shops from fall to spring. It is sold unwrapped and should be stored, wrapped in grease-proof paper, in a tightly closed box in the vegetable compartment of a refrigerator. It should be consumed as soon as possible after purchase.

Mascarpone

Milk:
🐄 🥛

Country of origin:
Italy

Recommended
drink:
Sparkling
white wine,
e.g. Prosecco

TYPE: Cream cheese

ORIGIN AND EXTENT: Mascarpone comes from Lombardy and is usually produced in the region around Lodi and Abbiategrasso.

FEATURES: Mascarpone is similar to raw-milk cheese and is offered either freely weighted or packed into containers closed in foil. The white-yellow cheese is creamy and can be greasy.

PRODUCTION: Mascarpone is produced by heating cream with a 30% fat content at 194°F. It is soured with lemon juice. Then the liquid is drained out and the mass is left to cool. The product is poured into containers for sale.

HISTORICAL NOTE: Formerly Mascarpone was prepared exclusively in autumn and in winter and was sold unpacked or in 3½ and 7 oz portions in small linen sacks. Today, thanks to modern cooling technology, it can be stored and consumed throughout the year. The origin of this cheese is unknown, but its preparation and use have been familiar for several centuries.

In the kitchen

Aroma:
Mascarpone has a mild, delicate flavor and smells of fresh cream.

Fat content:
60% fat in dry mass.

Use:
No authentic Tiramisu can be prepared without Mascarpone. It is an essential ingredient in many northern Italian sweet pastries and it is also used to improve the flavor of piquant dishes, such as sauces, pasta or risotto.

Purchase/Storage:
Mascarpone can be found in any larger supermarket. It should be stored in the refrigerator, especially after opening.

Mondseer

Milk:

Country of origin:
Austria

Recommended
drink:
White wine, e.g.,
green Valtellina

TYPE: sliced cheese

ORIGIN AND EXTENT: The home of this cheese is Mondseeland, in the western side of Salt Chamber.

FEATURES: Mondseer cheese weighs 2 lbs. The height of the edge is about 2 in and its rind is reddish and dry. The dough is firm and contains small holes.

PRODUCTION: Mondseer is produced from cows' milk. The cows producing the milk must not be fed with silage. The soured milk is cut into pea-sized pieces and put into molds. The cheese matures 4 to 6 weeks in cellars and is greased with red cultures and salt brine. Before packing, the red grease is removed and the rind is dried.

HISTORICAL NOTE: Mondseer, also known as Mondseer box cheese, has been known in the Salzburg area since 1818. It was probably first prepared in the castle of Hüttenstein, but the name Mondseer was given to the cheese in 1955. Until then, it was simply called box cheese.

IN THE KITCHEN

AROMA:
Mondseer has a piquant and spicy flavor.

FAT CONTENT:
45% fat in dry mass.

USE:
Mondseer is lovely with black peasant bread, a little bacon and tomatoes. It is suitable for cooking, but should be used sparingly due to its spicy flavor.

PURCHASE/STORAGE:
Mondseer can only be found in specialized cheese shops. In Austria, it is also available in small dairies. It can be stored for several days in the refrigerator, the whole piece tightly closed in a plastic case.

Montasio

Milk:
🐄 🥛

Country of origin:
Italy

Recommended
drink:
White wine, e.g.
Pinot Grigio

■ TYPE: Hard cheese

■ ORIGIN AND EXTENT: Montasio is produced in the Friaul/Julisch-Venice region, in the provinces of Belluno and Treviso and in parts of the provinces Padua and Venice.

■ FEATURES: Montasio is a round cheese with a height of 3 in, a diameter of 12 to 14 in and a weight between 13 to 18 lbs. Its rind is smooth and regular with a small number of holes. As a table cheese, it is compact with small holes and a natural, slightly straw-like color. As a grated table cheese, it is crumbly and straw-colored.

■ PRODUCTION: Montasio is produced exclusively from the milk of a maximum of four cows. The milk is soured by rennet and the curd is heated while stirring. After formation and pressing, the cheeses are salted, either dry or in brine. The period of maturation is 30 days at 46°F. Apportioning of the cheese is allowed only after a maturation period of at least 60 days, 2 to 5 months for a table cheese and at least 12 months for grated cheese.

In the kitchen

Aroma:

Montasio has an aromatic and spicy flavor. The longer the cheese matures, the stronger the flavor.

Fat content:

40% fat in dry mass.

Use:

Young Montasio is consumed with bread; mature cheese is preferable for baking.

Purchase/Storage:

Montasio can be found only in specialized cheese shops or in shops with Italian specialties. It can be stored, well-packed, in the vegetable box of a refrigerator.

Mont d'Or

Milk:

Country of
origin:
France

Recommended
drink:
White wine, e.g.
Riesling

■ TYPE: soft cheese with white mold

■ ORIGIN AND EXTENT: Mont d'Or, also known as Vacherin du Haut-Doubs, originates in eastern France near the Swiss between the Doubs, the Swiss border and the Doubs-Falls. The cows must be kept at a minimum height of 21,000 ft above sea-level.

■ FEATURES: This cheese can be recognized at first sight by the package. Mont d'Or is covered with a strip of spruce bark and is sold in a small sprucewood box. It is shaped like a small wheel and comes in various sizes. Its diameter ranges between 8 to 12 in; its height is 1 to 2 in and its weight lies between 1 to 7 lbs.

■ PRODUCTION: The milk for Mont d'Or comes exclusively from Monbéliard or Simmentaler cows. The cheese is still handmade, but only between 15 August and 31 March. The cheese matures in cellars on spruce boards. It is often turned over and doused with brine. After a minimum of 3 weeks of maturation, the cheese is packed in wooden boxes.

■ HISTORICAL NOTE: Cheese workshops have existed in the Haut-Doubs region since the 14th century. During that

time, Mont d'Or cheese production probably originated with farmers from the massif Mont d'Or. Under the protection of Saint-Claude abbey in the high mountain plateau of Jura, the land was fertilized. The establishment of the chalet system further developed cattle farming and milk production.

■■■ ANOTHER SORT OF MONT D'OR: Vacherin Mont d'Or of Switzerland, is prepared almost identically to Vacherin du Haut-Doubs. The cheese workshops producing this cheese

are situated on the Swiss side of Jura in the Lacs de Joux region. Therefore, the cheese is sometimes called Mont d'Or de Joux.

HAVE YOU TRIED...?

Mini-Fondue in a hurry: drench the cheese with small amount of white wine, wrap in aluminum foil and let it melt for about 10 minutes in the oven. Then cut off the cover and dip the crisp bread in the melted cheese. Enjoy this with a glass of red wine – could you wish for anything more?

IN THE KITCHEN

AROMA:

Mont d'Or has a lightly acidulous and bitter flavor which fills the mouth. It smells mildly of resin.

FAT CONTENT:

45% fat in dry mass.

USE:

Mont d'Or is usually bought in whole pieces and consumed directly with a spoon. It is suitable for baking and for flavoring soups and sauces.

PURCHASE/STORAGE:

Mont d'Or can be found in cheese shops. It can be kept for a short time, whole and wrapped, in the vegetable box of a refrigerator.

Morbier

Milk:

Country of origin:
France

Recommended drink:
White wine, e.g.
Sancerre

■ TYPE: sliced cheese

■ ORIGIN AND EXTENT: Morbier obtained the AOC impression after ten years of rigorous testing in 2001. Since that time, it has been subjected to strict production rules. The area of its production stretches across the departments Jura and Doubs and includes several villages in the departments Ain and Saône et Loire.

■ FEATURES: The mountain cheese Morbier is shaped like a water wheel with a diameter of 14 to 18 in and has a height of 2 to 3 in. Its weight ranges from 14 to 22 lbs. Its rind is pale gray to orange and matures naturally. Morbier can be distinguished from other mountain cheeses because it has a dark horizontal line caused by ash in its center.

■ PRODUCTION: According to AOC rules, only raw milk may be used in the production of Morbier. It comes from Monbéliard and Pie Rouge de l'Est cows, which are fed the grass and herbs in the mountain hayfields. The curd is heated and then pressed. The cheese must mature for at least 45 days at the temperature 45° to 59°F, but it may mature for up to 9 weeks. The longer the cheese matures, the milder and creamier it is.

IN THE KITCHEN

AROMA:
Morbier is scentless. Its flavor is mild and slightly reminiscent of the country and hay.

FAT CONTENT:
45% fat in dry mass.

USE:
Morbier is preferably served on strong peasant bread. It is also served in warm dishes and can be used for baking.

PURCHASE/STORAGE:
Morbier can be found on cheese stands and in specialized shops. It can be stored whole, if well-packed, in the refrigerator. It should not be stored a long time after purchase.

DO YOU KNOW THAT...?

The ash line originates from the beginning of the history of Morbier 200 years ago. During the winter months, farmers from distant yards could not deliver milk to dairies because of the large amounts of snow. The quantity of milk was so small that it was not possible to make a whole cheese from one milking. To prevent the formation of a crust on the morning milk, they spread ash on it and in the evening, added the sour from the second milking. Today, vegetable ash is used for this purpose.

Mozzarella

Milk:
🐄 🥛

Origin:
Italy

Recommended
drink:
White wine
e.g.Pinot Grigio

▬ TYPE: Filata-cheese

▬ ORIGIN AND EXTENT: Mozzarella originated in Italy, but now it is produced all over the world. "Mozzarella di bufala campana" comes from Campania or Latium.

▬ FEATURES: The common shape of Mozzarella is a ball, but another shapes, known throughout the cheese producing-region, are "Bocconcini," or "mouthfuls," "Ciliegine," "small cherries," and "Nodini," "small knots." For gastronomical purposes, either small or large cheeses are produced. The weight ranges between 7 oz and 1¾ lbs, depending on the shape. Its color is porcelain white. Its rind is very thin and smooth. The cheese is mildly elastic and its consistency is homogenous.

▬ PRODUCTION: The milk is heated between 91° to 97°F and soured by the addition of rennet and fermented milk. The curd is then cut into hazelnut-sized pieces. It matures in whey for five hours. Then the mass is cut into strips and poured into special containers, where, after adding water heated to 203°F, it is cut to the required shape and size. It is subsequently cooled in cold water, salted in pickle brine and shaped.

▬ VARIANTS: *Mozzarella di bufala campana* is produced

exclusively from buffalo milk. The buffalo herds must originate in a specific Mediterranean region and be registered in the local cattle registry and raised according to local tradition. The milk should be delivered to cheese dairies 16 hours after milking with a fat content at least 7%.

Mozzarella di bufala campana affumicata. The term "affumicata" means "smoked." Mozzarella may be smoked only by natural and traditional procedures.

Baked Mozzarella-Crostini

■ INGREDIENTS: 8 slices of white bread• 11 oz Mozzarella
• 2 eggs • sunflower oil • flour • salt and pepper

■ PREPARATION: Beat the eggs and add salt and pepper.
Cut the Mozzarella into thin slices and sprinkle with flour. Lay
the white bread slices and the Mozzarella in the egg mixture,
put one slice of Mozzarella between two slices of bread, coat
them with the flour and fry in hot oil.

IN THE KITCHEN

AROMA:
Mozzarella has a mildly acidulous flavor.

FAT CONTENT:
45% fat in dry mass.

USE:
Insalata Caprese, which combines raw Mozzarella, tomatoes, basilica, pepper and olive oil is a classic dish, but small balls pickled with herbs, garlic and oil make an excellent hors d'oeuvre. For baking pizza or as ingredient in pasta dishes, Mozzarella is the preferred cheese. Classical Margherita pizza cannot be prepared without Mozzarella.

PURCHASE/STORAGE:
Mozzarella can be found wrapped in foil in the cool box of any discount food store. Mozzarella di bufala, however, can be obtained only in special shops. Once open, the packet can only be stored in the refrigerator for a few days.

Munster

Milk:
🐄 🥛

Country of origin:
France

Recommended
drink:
White wine, e.g.
spicy Tramine

■ TYPE: Soft cheese with washed rind

■ ORIGIN AND EXTENT: The home of this cheese is the Vosges in eastern France. The world famous cheese, bearer of the AOC–impression, may be produced in only seven departments: Bas-Rhin, Haut-Rhin, Vosges, Meurthe-et-Moselle, Moselle, Haute Saône and Territoire de Belfort.

■ FEATURES: The soft cheese has a washed rind with red cultures. It is available in two sizes. The first has a round shape, a diameter of 5 to 8 in and a height of 1 to 3 in. The weight is at least 16 oz, but must not exceed 3 lb. The second one is called Petit Munster. Its weight is at least 4 oz, its diameter is 3 to 5 in and it has a height of 1 to 2 in. The yellow dough is creamy and supple.

■ PRODUCTION: Munster is made from cow's milk. The milk is soured by adding rennet. The curd is neither washed nor kneaded, but is put into molds and the whey slowly drained. Then the mixture is removed from molds and salted. Munster must mature at least 21 days. Petit Munster may leave the cellar after 14 days. During its maturation, Munster is turned over and rinsed every 2 days.

■■■ HISTORICAL NOTE: Like many other French cheeses, Munster was invented by monks. In the year 660, Benedictine monks founded a monastery in Alsace and a new village quickly rose around it. This village was named Munster. The monks looked for the best pastures in Vosges to supply their kitchen. They gradually pushed further and further west and allowed their pigs to pasture in Lothringen on the other side of the mountains. In 1285, the Alsatians and the Lotharingians founded a new town by the name Sancti Gerardi Mare, later changed by the people to Gérardmer, pronounced Géromé. Soon the

Lotharingians learned to prepare the cheese and produced the same cheese, but called it Géromé. So the same cheese is called Munster in Alsace, but Géromé in Lothringen. Both cheeses bear the AOC–impression.

Potatoes with Munster

■ INGREDIENTS: 3 lbs new potatoes • 1 onion • 1 clove of garlic • 5 oz boiled ham • 2 sprigs of parsley • 1 sprig of savory • 7 oz Munster • 1 – 1½ tablespoons butter • 1 tablespoon sunflower oil • salt, pepper and mace

■ PREPARATION: Cut the potatoes into thin slices, roast on the butter and oil until golden brown for about 25 minutes, add the chopped onion with the minced clove of garlic, and some salt, pepper and mace. Roast together for 5 minutes. Cut the ham into strips, chop the herbs and mix with the potatoes. Fill the soufflé mold with the mixture, put thick slices of Munster on the surface and bake in the preheated oven under a grill. Crisp green salad completes this dish.

In the kitchen

Aroma:
Munster has a distinctive smell and a powerful, spicy, salty flavor. The more mature the cheese, the stronger and spicier its aroma.

Fat content:
45% fat in dry mass.

Use:
Munster is served with peasant bread containing caraway. Regional specialties include unpeeled potatoes, omelet or quiche made with Munster.

Purchase/storage:
Munster can be found at cheese stands or in specialized cheese shops. For a few days, it can be stored whole, wrapped in grease-proof paper and tightly enclosed in a plastic box, in the vegetable compartment of a refrigerator.

Neufchatel

■ TYPE: Soft cheese with white mold

■ ORIGIN AND EXTENT: This cheese originates from Boutonnière du Pays de Bray, a narrow plateau protected against winds by the limestone rocks of Haute-Normandy. The cheese possesses the AOC-impression and may only come from the Seine-Maritime department in eastern Normandy.

■ FEATURES: Neufchatel is covered by the downy, white rind of the mold. It is available in six variants. Peasants sell homemade Neufchatel on straw sheets. The cheese from the dairy is packed in paper.

■ PRODUCTION: The cow's milk is soured with rennet for a period of 24 to 36 hours. Then the curd is slightly pressed to enable the whey to drain quickly. The cheese curd is then mixed with small pieces of the mature cheese, covered with white mold and mixed until the mass becomes homogenous. Then the cheese mass is shaped and salted before maturing for 10 to 12 days in a cellar.

Milk:

Country of origin:
France

Recommended drink:
Apple wine,
e.g. Cider

In the kitchen

Aroma:
Neufchatel has a delicate piquant and acidulous flavor reminiscent of mushrooms.

Fat content:
45% fat in dry mass.

Use:
This heart-shaped cheese is distinctive on any cheese plate. It is hardly ever used for cooking.

Purchase/storage:
Neufchatel can be found in cheese shops. It

should be refrigerated whole, wrapped in grease-proof paper and enclosed in a plastic box, in the vegetable compartment of the refrigerator.

Variants:

The heart-shaped cheese is 4 in wide with a height of 1½ in. The larger version of the heart cheese is 1 in larger in all its dimensions. The cylindrical cheese has a diameter of 2 in and a height of almost 3 in. The double cylindrical cheese is 3 in higher and its diameter is 2 in. The square cheese has 10 in edges and a height of 1 in. The oblong cheese has a length of 3 in, a width of 2 in and a height of 1 in.

Ossau-Iraty Brebis-Pyrénées

TYPE: Sliced cheese

ORIGIN AND EXTENT: Ossau-Iraty Brebis-Pyrénées originates in the Béarn region and the Basque country in the Pyrénées-Atlantiques department as well as in a small part of Hautes-Pyrénées in southwestern France.

FEATURES: Ossau-Iraty Brebis-Pyrénées is a flat or slightly convex cylinder with a diameter of 10 in and a height of 5 to 5½ in. Its weight ranges from 9 to 11 lbs. If homemade, it may weigh up to 15 lbs. A smaller variant, Petit Ossau-Iraty, reaches a weight of 4 to 7 lbs. The cheese has a thick, orange-yellow to gray rind and smooth, white curd with a firm consistency.

PRODUCTION: Ossau-Iraty Brebis-Pyrénées is produced traditionally. The sheep's milk is soured by rennet; it is then stirred, manually poured into molds and pressed. The cheeses are salted with coarse salt and matured for at least 3 months at temperatures below 54°F with relative air humidity above 80%.

IN THE KITCHEN

AROMA:
Ossau-Iraty Brebis-Pyrénées cheese has a nutty and plant-like flavor and an aroma subtly reminiscent of sheep.

FAT CONTENT:
50% fat in dry mass.

USE:
In France, Ossau-Iraty Brebis-Pyrénées is traditionally consumed by shepherds and peasants for brunch. When the cheese is more mature, it is suitable for grating and can be used in soufflés and as an ingredient in soups.

PURCHASE/STORAGE:
Ossau-Iraty Brebis-Pyrénées can only be found in specialized cheese shops. The best time to find Ossau-Iraty Brebis-Pyrénées is in early spring and fall. If this cheese is packed well, it can be stored in the refrigerator for a long time.

DID YOU KNOW THAT...?

The name, Ossau-Iraty Brebis-Pyrénées, recalls both the province of Béarn and the Pays Basque, a mostly mountainous country with many deep valleys and forests. The area receives much rain and the Mancch and Basco-Béarnaise sheep have been raised there for centuries. Ossau-Iraty Brebis-Pyrénées has a long history.

Parmigiano Reggiano

Milk:
🐄 🥛

Country of origin:
Italy

Recommended
drink:
Red wine, e.g.
Lambrusco

■ TYPE: Hard cheese

■ ORIGIN AND EXTENT: Parmigiano Reggiano is a world famous cheese under the name, Parmesan. The cheese with AOC–impression is produced exclusively in the provinces of Bologna, Modena, Parma, Reggio Emilia and Montova.

■ FEATURES: Parmigiano Reggiano has a cylindrical shape with a slightly convex margin. Its diameter is 14 to 18 in and has a height of 7 to 9 in. It weighs at least 53 lb, the rind is of natural yellow color and is about ¹⁄₁₀ in thick. The straw-colored cheese has a mildly grainy consistency, but is crumbly to cut.

■ PRODUCTION: Parmigiano Reggiano is produced from cow's milk. The cows were fed from the meadows in the area of origin. Silage and fermented feed is forbidden. For cheese production, the milk drawn during the evening is partially skimmed and mixed with the morning milk. After the addition of natural whey, rich in lactic acid bacteria, rennet is also added. The curd is cut into small grains and is heated. No other ingredients may be added. After several days, the cheese is salted for 20 to 25 days. Then the cheese must mature for at least 12 months. The optimal time for maturity is 20 to 24 months.

■ STAGES OF MATURITY: *Giovane or fresco:* After 14 months of maturation, it may be called "fresh" Parmigiano Reggiano.

Vecchio: After 18 to 24 months, it is known as Parmigiano Reggiano "vecchio," which means "old."

Stravecchio is a fully mature Parmigiano Reggiano which has matured for 2 to 3 years.

Stravecchione Parmigiano Reggiano is the name used after the cheese has matured for 3 to 4 years, meaning, obviously, "extra old."

Green lasagne with Pesto

■ INGREDIENTS: 1 bunch of basil • 3 cloves of garlic • ½ cup grated Parmesan • 2 tablespoons pine nuts • 1 cup olive oil • salt and pepper • 3½ tablespoons butter • 3½ tablespoons flour • 2 cups milk • 1 lb green leaves of lasagne

■ PREPARATION: Pare and press the garlic, mince with the basil, 5 tablespoons Parmesan and the pine nuts in a mixer. Carefully add the oil and then the salt and pepper.

For the preparation of the Béchamel, heat the butter in a pan until foaming, add the flour and dilute with milk. Bring to a boil while stirring. Add salt and pepper to taste. Mix two thirds of the Béchamel with pesto and with several spoonfuls of the noodle water. Grease the bottom of the soufflé mold with butter and put three leaves of lasagna there, greased with a little pesto-Béchamel mixture. Spread a little Parmesan and a few flakes of butter over the whole and continue until all the leaves of lasagna are used. Mix the remaining parmesan with the Béchamel and pour it over the surface, adding more flakes of butter. Let it cool for six hours and then bake in the oven at 392°F for 25 to 30 minutes.

IN THE KITCHEN

AROMA:
Parmigiano Reggiano has a spicy, piquant, but not sharp, flavor.

FAT CONTENT:
32% fat in dry mass.

USE:
Parmigiano Reggiano is most commonly grated and added to pasta, soups and other dishes. It can also be flaked over salads, a classical addition to Bresaola or Carpaccio. It mixes well with fine Mozzarella or with other less pungently flavored cheeses. In Italy, small pieces of this cheese are served as canapés.

PURCHASE/STORAGE:
Parmigiano Reggiano can be found refrigerated in supermarkets and also on cheese stands. It should always be bought whole and grated at home to preserve the strong aroma and to ensure a longer shelf life. Wrapped in grease-proof paper and aluminum foil, it can be stored for 1 to 2 months.

Passendale

Milk:
🐄 🥛

Country of origin:
Belgium

Recommended
drink:
Red wine, e.g.
Dornfelder

▬ TYPE: Semi-hard, sliced cheese

▬ ORIGIN AND EXTENT: The home of Passendale is west Flanders in Belgium where it is regarded as a peasant cheese.

▬ FEATURES: Passendale has a shape and size similar to peasant bread. It weighs about 7 lb. The rind is dark yellow and slightly covered by white mold. The egg-yolk yellow cheese is supple and usually perforated.

▬ PRODUCTION: Passendale is produced from pasteurized cow's milk soured by rennet and cut up. After the curd is cut, it is formed and salt is added. Then the cheese matures at least 45 days in mildly humid air.

IN THE KITCHEN

AROMA:
The flavor of Passendale ranges from mildly spicy to piquant.

FAT CONTENT:
50% fat in dry mass.

USE:
Passendale is a delightful accompaniment to bread. It can also be used for gratinating vegetables such as asparagus, broccoli or chicory. The young cheese is favored by children while connoisseurs prefer more mature cheese.

PURCHASE/STORAGE:
Passendale can be found in any larger cheese stand or in specialized cheese shops. It can be stored in a refrigerator if wellpacked in grease-proof paper and aluminum foil.

Pecorino Romano

Milk:
🐑 🥛

Country of origin:
Italy

Recommended
drink:
Red wine, e.g.
Chianti classico

▬ TYPE: Hard cheese

▬ ORIGIN AND EXTENT: Pecorino Romano is produced in the regions of Sardinia and Latium as well as in the province of Grosseto.

▬ FEATURES: Pecorino Romano has the shape of a tall cylinder with a diameter of 10 to 14 in. The weight ranges between 44 to 77 lbs. Its thin, ivory or straw-colored rind is sometimes covered by a protective layer. The structure of the white or pale yellow cheese is compact with very few holes.

▬ PRODUCTION: The cheese is produced exclusively from raw sheep's milk. Salting is dry or accomplished through a pickling process. The period of maturation lasts at least 5 months for table cheese and 8 months for grating cheese. In some cases, the cheese is covered by a neutral or black protective layer. Traditionally, the cheese is produced from October to July.

▬ HISTORICAL NOTE: It is probable that the ancient Romans consumed Pecorino. The name "Pecorino" comes from Italian word "pecora," or "sheep." All Italian hard cheeses made of sheep's milk are called Pecorino.

■ VARIANTS: *Pecorino siciliano:* This sheep's cheese comes from Sicily and is flavored by black pepper. Thus its flavor is extra sharp.

Pecorino toscano: This sheep's cheese comes from Tuscany and is usually consumed before maturity. It has a soft, creamy structure.

Pecorino sienese: Another sort of Pecorino toscano. Tomato purée is rubbed into its rind.

Salat alla Medici

■ INGREDIENTS: 1 lb mixed salad leaves (Romana, Frisée, Radicchio, Rucola) • 6 spring onions • 4 sardines in oil • 3½ tablespoons capers • 3 tablespoons olive oil • 1 tablespoon red vinegar • salt and pepper • 2 tablespoons cracked walnuts • 14 oz Pecorino

■ PREPARATION: Wash and dry salad leaves, cut the onion into small slices. Mince the sardines and drain the capers. Put all the ingredients into a salad dish. Mix a marinade of oil, vinegar, salt and pepper and add to salad, tossing thoroughly. Cut the Pecorino into thin slices and put on the salad, together with the chopped walnuts. Serve with Ciabatta bread.

IN THE KITCHEN

AROMA:

Pecorino Romano as a table cheese is aromatic, salty and slightly piquant. The more mature the grating cheese, the harder it becomes, but it does not have a very intense flavor.

FAT CONTENT:

36% fat in dry mass.

USE:

Young Pecorino is consumed with Ciabatta or sliced into the thinnest slices and eaten with a glass of wine. In its grated form, it is added to soups and pasta.

PURCHASE/STORAGE

Pecorino Romano can be found in cheese shops or in Italian specialty shops. It can be stored in the refrigerator for 1 to 2 months if well-packed.

Pélardon

Milk:

Country of origin:
France

Recommended
drink:
Red wine,
e.g. Coteaux du
Languedoc

■ TYPE: soft cheese

■ ORIGIN AND EXTENT: The home of Pélardon is in the Languedoc-Roussillon region. The area of production covers the departments Gard, Hérault, Aude, Lozère and Tarn.

■ FEATURES: Pélardon has a fine, ivory-colored rind which may be covered by white and blue mold after a long period of maturation. When the cheese is young, it is soft and creamy. Older cheese becomes crumbly. The round cheese has a diameter of 2 to 3 in and a height of ½ to 1 in. It weighs about 2 oz.

■ PRODUCTION: Pélardon is produced exclusively from raw goats' milk. After souring, the curd is poured into molds with a ladle. When the whey has been drained, the cheese is salted and matures at least 11 days.

■ HISTORICAL NOTE: Formerly, goat cheese was a staple of the rural peasant diet and a popular commodity at country markets. Today, it is more widely enjoyed, but has preserved its peasant character.

IN THE KITCHEN

AROMA:

Young Pélardon has a nutty flavor. During its maturity, this flavor becomes stronger. It may also possess an aroma of flowers and honey.

FAT CONTENT:

45% fat in dry mass.

USE:

Pélardon is not only served at the end of the menu, but also as an hors d'oeuvre. Like other goat cheeses, it is suitable for frying and is used to flavor lamb and beef sauces.

PURCHASE/STORAGE:

Pélardon can be found in cheese shops. If well packed, it can be stored whole for several days in the vegetable box of a refrigerator.

DO YOU KNOW THAT...?

Pélardon has preserved its old, rustic character because the goats are still raised naturally and the production is often completed manually in farmhouses.

Pico

Milk:
🐄 🥛

Country of origin:
Portugal

Recommended
drink:
Dessert wine,
e.g. Madeira

■ TYPE: soft cheese

■ ORIGIN AND EXTENT: The cheese comes from Pico, one of the Azores Islands. Monte Pico, the tallest mountain of Azores, reaching 1½ miles high, is located there.

■ FEATURES: Pico is light yellow colored and has a soft consistency. The round cheese usually weighs 1 to 2 lbs, has a diameter of 7 in and a height of approximately 1 in.

■ PRODUCTION: Pico is produced from raw cow's milk. After the creation of the curd, the whey is left to drain freely. After salting, it matures for 15 days.

■ HISTORICAL NOTE: The Atlantic climate of the Azores and Madeira enables the raising of cows and the production of milk and cheese. On the Portuguese mainland, cheese is still produced from sheep and goat's milk. Sailors taught the inhabitants of the islands to produce the cheese. It is not known how cows first arrived on the islands.

In the kitchen

Aroma:
Pico has a slightly salty, but mild flavor.

Fat content:
45% fat in dry mass.

Use:
Pico harmonizes well with other cheeses on cheese plates.

Purchase/storage:
Pico can be found in cheese shops or in shops that carry Portuguese specialties. It should be stored whole, well packed in the vegetable box of a refrigerator.

Picodon

■ TYPE: soft cheese

■ ORIGIN AND EXTENT: The home of Picodon lies in the Ardèche and Drôme Mountains. Since it is an AOC-cheese, its origin is strictly limited to the southern Rhône area, which consists of Ardèche and Drôme, canton Barjac in the department of Gard and canton Valréas in the department of Vaucluse.

■ FEATURES: Picodon is formed in sheets with a thickness of ½ to 1 in. The cheese is fine, homogenous and firmer after maturing. The cheese is covered by a natural layer of mold. The longer the cheese matures, the more visible the blue mold and red flora. Picodon is sold unwrapped.

■ PRODUCTION: Picodon is produced from goat's milk and is soured by adding a very small amount of rennet. The curd is transferred by ladles to perforated molds. After the whey is drained, the curd is salted and dried on grates and then the cheese matures for at least 12 days. When Picodon has matured for 1 month, it enters a new phase, referred to by specialists as "Dieulefit-Affinage" during which the cheese is washed several times with salt brine and rubbed with wine or brandy.

IN THE KITCHEN

AROMA:
Young Picodon has a mild, slightly salty flavor. During the period of maturation, it becomes nutty. It is possible to smell a fine goat odor.

FAT CONTENT:
45% fat in dry mass.

USE:
Picodon is not only served as a last course, but is consumed for brunch in its home region. The cheese can be grilled or served with various salads. Picodon can be also pickled in white wine, fruit brandy or olive oil.

PURCHASE/STORAGE:
Picodon can be found in cheese shops. It can be stored whole, well-packed in the vegetable box of a refrigerator.

Pont-l'Evêque

Milk:
🐄 🥛

Country of origin:
France

Recommended
drink:
Red wine,
e.g. Burgundy

■ TYPE: soft cheese with washed rind

■ ORIGIN AND EXTENT: Pont-l'Evque is named after a village between Lisieux and Deauville. The cheese is protected by an AOC-impression and can only be produced in five departments: Calvados, Eure, Manche, Orne and Seine-Maritime in Normandy and Mayenne in Pays-de-la-Loire.

■ FEATURES: Pont-l'Evèque is a cheese with a square shape and a washed and brushed orange-yellow rind. It comes in four sizes. The height is always 1 in and the edges are usually 4 to 4 ½ in. The weight ranges from ½ to 1 lb. In dairies, the cheese is divided into halves before the maturation is completed. The smaller variant, Petit Pont-l'Evèque, has edges measuring 3 to 4 in and the edge of the larger variant, Grand Pont-l'Evèque, is about 7½ to 8 in.

■ PRODUCTION: Pont-l'Evèque was traditionally produced from cow's milk in the old province of Normandy. Due to the increased demand for cheese, the area of milk collection was enlarged. The warm milk is treated with rennet. The curd is then cut and put into molds. After the cheese is salted, it is stored for 4 to 6 weeks in cellars to mature. The cheeses are rubbed repeatedly with brine.

━━━ HISTORICAL NOTE: Pont-l'Evèque was known in the Middle Ages as "Angelon" or "Angelot." Also in the 16th century, it was called "Augelot," in reference to its origin in the Pays d'Auge. The cheese obtained its current name in the 17th century.

Spinach nests

■ INGREDIENTS: 1 to 1½ lbs spinach (frozen) • salt • 1 onion • 4 tablespoons olive oil • 2 tablespoons sun-dried tomatoes in oil • 4 pickled artichoke hearts • pepper • 1 teaspoon Provencal herbs • 2 tablespoons pine nuts • 7 oz Pont-l'Evèque

■ PREPARATION: Defrost the spinach in a little salted water and pour out the water. Cut the onion into small squares, fry them in 2 tablespoons olive oil until they turn a pale color. Cut the sun-dried tomatoes and artichoke hearts into thin slices and stew briefly in the mixture. Add salt, pepper and herbs. Add pine nuts, about 4 tablespoons oil and the sun-dried tomatoes and mix thoroughly. Grease four little molds with oil and divide the spinach into them and cover each with tomato mixture. Cut the cheese into thin slices and cover the spinach nests. Drip the remaining oil onto the nests and gratinate them in preheated oven for 15 to 20 minutes at 392°F.

IN THE KITCHEN

AROMA:
The smell of older Pont-l'Evèque is rather pungent, but mild when the cheese is still young.

FAT CONTENT:
45% fat in dry mass.

USE:
Sliced Pont-l'Evèque is good with bread, but it can also be baked in potato and vegetable dishes.

PURCHASE/STORAGE:
Pont-l'Evèque can be found in cheese shops. It can be stored for several days wrapped in grease-proof paper and enclosed in a plastic case in the vegetable box of a refrigerator.

Pouligny Saint-Pierre

Pronunciation:
Pulini Sain pier

Milk:

Country of origin:
France

Recommended
drink:
White wine,
e.g. Pouilly-Fumé
or Sancerre

TYPE: soft cheese

ORIGIN AND EXTENT: The home of Pouligny Saint-Pierre is in the western part of the Indre department and the middle of the Loire.

FEATURES: The most distinctive feature of this cheese is its pyramid shape. The length of the edge at the foot is 3½ in, 1 in on the top and the height is 5 in. The weight is about ½ lb. The smaller variant is Petit Pouligny Saint-Pierre. Its dimensions are strictly prescribed: 3 x 1 x 3½ in.

PRODUCTION: For the production of Pouligny Saint-Pierre, goat's milk is soured with rennet. The curd is poured into pyramid shaped molds. After draining, formation and salting, the cheese is dried on wooden gratings or straw boards. The period of maturation can last at least 2 weeks, but usually takes 4 to 5 weeks.

HAVE YOU TRIED ...?

Prepare a salad from endive and rucola with vinaigrette. Put the cheese on toasted slices of white bread and place them under a grill. When finished, add salad and spread with cracked pine kernels.

IN THE KITCHEN

AROMA:
Young Pouligny Saint-Pierre has a mild, slightly acidulous flavor. During maturation, the flavor becomes nutty. Mostly only mature cheese is offered.

FAT CONTENT:
45% fat in dry mass.

USE:
Pouligny Saint-Pierre is suitable for cheese plates. It is also well-suited for salads with walnut oil dressing. It can be served sliced and lightly gratinated on white bread.

PURCHASE/STORAGE:
Pouligny Saint-Pierre can be found in cheese shops. The best Pouligny Saint-Pierre can be obtained from early spring to late fall, when the goats pasture in lush meadows. It can be stored for several days, well-packed, in the vegetable box of a refrigerator.

Provolone valpadana

Milk:
🐄 📦

Country of origin:
Italy

Recommended drink:
Red wine,
e.g. Bararesco

■ TYPE: Filata-cheese

■ ORIGIN AND EXTENT: Provolone is produced throughout the Cremona and Brescia provinces as well as in several villages in the provinces of Bergamo, Mantua, Milan, Verona, Vicenza, Rovigo, Padua and Piacenza and several villages in the province of Trento.

■ FEATURES: Provolone can be found in any number of shapes including salami, melon, skittle or pear. The weight of Provolone varies from 1 to 220 ½ lb. The cheese, which can be eaten after only a short maturation period, weighs between 1 and 13 lb. All Provolone cheeses have a smooth, thin rind which is golden yellow, or sometimes yellow-brown. The straw-colored dough is compact and sometimes shows small, scarcely discernable holes.

■ PRODUCTION: For the production of Provolone, cows' milk is soured by adding rennet. The curd is cut up, washed with whey and molded. The molding is done manually or by means of special molds and then the formed pieces are placed in a salt brine for 12 hours or 25 days, depending on the shape. Small cheeses mature for 3 months, larger cheeses take much longer. Provolone can also be smoked.

IN THE KITCHEN

AROMA:
Provolone has a mild flavor until it matures for three months. When the time of maturation is longer, or when goat and/or sheep rennet is used, the flavor is much more intense.

FAT CONTENT:
44% fat in dry mass.

USE:
Due to its excellent melting qualities, the cheese is suitable for preparing soufflé dishes. It is also served raw with bread or lightly grilled as an intermediate course.

PURCHASE/STORAGE:
Provolone can be found in cheese shops or in Italian specialty shops. It can be stored whole, well-packed, in the vegetable box of a refrigerator.

Quark

Milk:
🐄 🥛

Country of origin:
Germany

▬ TYPE: Curd cheese

▬ ORIGIN AND EXTENT: Germans during the Stone Age made curd cheese and its preparation spread to the Northern Alpine countries. It has been produced industrially since the 19th century and is also known as Topfen.

▬ FEATURES: Quark is a white, creamy mass packed tightly in closed plastic containers and weighs between ½ to 3 lbs.

▬ PRODUCTION: For the production of Quark, pasteurized, skimmed milk is soured by lactic acid bacteria. The liquid is removed from the mass in a centrifuge and then the curds are pressed and a smooth mass obtained. Quark doesn't need to mature. It contains about 80% water and is sold with various fat contents. For half-fat or full fat variations, cream is added.

▬ SIMILAR TYPES: *Layer cheese* is produced when the curds are not centrifuged. It is put into molds in layers and the whey is left to drain.
Fresh cream cheese or double cream cheese is prepared similarly to Quark, but much more liquid is removed during souring. It is salted and cream is added to adjust fat content.

Grainy fresh cottage cheese is produced when the curds are slightly heated, contracting the milk proteins into small grains. After the whey is drained, the cheese must be washed with cold water to keep the mass grainy, but not sticky.

Curd cheese cake

▬ INGREDIENTS: 4 eggs • 1 cup sugar • 9 oz butter • 1 packet of baking powder • 1 packet of vanilla sugar • 1 packet of vanilla pudding powder • 4 tablespoons semolina • 1 untreated lemon • 3 lb Quark • 1 can mandarin oranges

▬ PREPARATION: Beat eggs with sugar until they foam, add butter in flakes at room temperature and mix well. Then add baking powder, vanilla sugar and pudding powder, semolina and grated lemon peel. Mix well with Quark. Grease a cake tin with a diameter of 10 in, spread with breadcrumbs, put drained mandarin oranges on the bottom and fill the tin with the curds mass. Bake in the oven at 392°F for about 1 hour. When the baking is finished, let the cake rest for another 15 minutes in the open oven.

HAVE YOU TRIED...?

Spunde cheese: Mix 9 oz fat-free Quark with 7 tablespoons double cream fresh cheese and tablespoons soft butter into a homogenous mass. Flavor the mass with 1 teaspoon paprika powder, salt and a pinch of sugar. Chop two red onions into fine pieces. Spunde cheese is served with chopped onion and small salted pretzels. First, dip the pretzel in Spunde cheese and then in onion. Consume with a glass of white wine.

IN THE KITCHEN

AROMA:
Quark has a neutral scent and slightly acidulous flavor.

FAT CONTENT:
0.5% fat absolute.

USE:
Quark has many uses in the kitchen. When cold, it can be flavored with herbs or simply spread on bread with jam. It can be an ingredient in cooking, added to salads, baked into cheese cakes or sweet soufflés and used in the preparation of curds dough.

PURCHASE/STORAGE:
Quark can be found refrigerated in any discount shop or supermarket. Once opened, it can be stored, tightly-closed, for a few days in the refrigerator.

DID YOU KNOW THAT...?

The word "Quark" is derived from the medieval German terms "twarc" or "zwarc." In the 14th century, the prefix "qu" was added. Both terms were probably taken from the Slavic stock of words. In Eastern Europe, "zwarc" was considered the favorite dish of slaves. Today, children love curd cheese with fruit.

Raclette

Milk:
🐄 🥛

Country of origin:
Switzerland

Recommended
drink:
White wine,
e.g. Fendant

▬ TYPE: Hard cheese

▬ ORIGIN AND EXTENT: This cheese originated in Wallis, but today it is produced in the northern Alpine ridge in Switzerland.

▬ FEATURES: Round or squared cheese weighs 12 to 16½ lbs. Its diameter or edge length is 12 to 14 in. The rind is brownish red and the light yellow or ivory-colored cheese is fine and slightly creamy.

▬ PRODUCTION: Raclette is still made from raw milk in mountain chalets, but in dairies in the valley, it usually comes from pasteurized milk. The milk is heated and soured by rennet. The curd is cut by a wire knife into small pieces and the whey is separated from the cheese mass. The mass is heated again while stirring and then pressed into molds. After being removed from the molds, the cheeses are salted and mature at least three months before they are offered for sale.

▬ HISTORICAL NOTE: The name "La Raclette" probably comes from the French word "racler," meaning "scratch" or "scrape."

IN THE KITCHEN

AROMA:
Raclette has a spicy and lightly acidulous flavor.

FAT CONTENT:
45% fat in dry mass.

USE:
Because of its excellent melting capacity, Raclette is suitable for eating on toast, soufflé and grilled meats.

PURCHASE/STORAGE:
Raclette can be found in any larger cheese stand. Store the cheese alone or with cheeses of the same type in grease-proof paper and perforated foil in a refrigerator set at 50° F.

DID YOU KNOW THAT...?

Raclette is a Swiss cheese with a rich heritage and a favorite Swiss dish. As early as the Middle Ages, shepherds enjoyed spicy Raclette. To increase the spiciness, they heated half a loaf over the fire and scraped the fused cheese.

Reblochon de Savoie

■ TYPE: Semi-hard, sliced cheese

■ ORIGIN AND EXTENT: The origin of Reblochon lis in Haute-Savoie, in the Pays de Thônes mountains. The AOC-impression guarantees that this cheese comes from French Rhône-Alpes region south of Lake Leman.

■ FEATURES: Reblochon has a washed rind, covered by natural noble mold. The cheese has a flat rounded shape with a diameter of 5½ in and a height of 1½ in. Its weight is 1 lb. The smaller variant, Petit Reblochon de Savoie, has a diameter of only 3 in and a height of about 1 in. Its weight ranges from 8 to 10 oz. Reblochon is presented on a disk made of imitation pine wood.

■ PRODUCTION: Raw cow's milk from three local cows is used to produce every Reblochon. It is forbidden to feed the cows silage. The cheese is produced by means of rennet. The curd is put into molds and lightly pressed. During the 2 weeks of maturation, the rind is washed several times.

IN THE KITCHEN

AROMA:
Reblochon smells of the cellar and has a buttery flavor.

FAT CONTENT:
45% fat in dry mass.

USE:
This cheese is ideal for breakfast sandwiches, but is also great on a cheese plate.

PURCHASE / STORAGE:
Reblochon can be found in specialized cheese shops. It should be stored whole, wrapped in grease-proof paper enclosed in a plastic case in the vegetable box of a refrigerator.

DID YOU KNOW THAT...?

This cheese appeared in the 14th century. Farmers paid their rent in milk products. When the milk supply was low, the farmer milked his cows only partially. After the rent collector left, the farmer finished milking. This very creamy additional milk was used for the production of Reblochon.

Ricotta

Milk:

Country of origin:
Italy

Recommended
drink:
Dessert wine,
e.g. Marsala

■ TYPE: Fresh cheese

■ ORIGIN AND EXTENT: Ricotta was overshadowed by other cheeses for a long time because it is produced from whey, the waste product of cheese production. It is made throughout the cheese-producing areas of Italy.

■ FEATURES: Ricotta is snow-white and its structure is soft and slightly crumbly. It may be pressed into blocks or baskets, or in containers as curds.

■ PRODUCTION: Ricotta is not produced from milk, but from whey. To be soured, the whey must be heated to 158 to 176°F. The mass is heated once more to enable the liquid to be separated. The fresh Ricotta is then put in baskets, allowing the remaining liquid to drain. Then it is removed from baskets, briefly pressed and packed without any maturation time.

■ HISTORICAL NOTE: In antiquity, Ricotta was made from the whey of goat and sheep's milk. The name "Ricotta" means "cooked again" and denotes the method of production.

■■■ VARIANT: *Ricotta romana* is the most favored Ricotta in middle and southern Italy and it is produced from the whey of sheep's milk, a by-product of the production of Pecorino.

Ricotta di vacca or *Ricotta vaccine*, the attributes "di vacca" or "vaccina," signify that this cheese was produced from the whey of cow's milk.

■■■ SORTS: The designation "Ricotta tipo dolce" means, that the cheese is unsalted. The designation "Ricotta tipo forte" signifies that the cheese has matured. "Ricotta salata" declares the cheese salted and "affumicata" means that the cheese has been smoked. The designation "Ricotta secca" means that this is a hard cheese for grating.

Ricotta walnut cake

INGREDIENTS: 10½ tablespoons walnuts • 5 oz butter • 10½ tablespoons sugar • 5 eggs • 1 lemon peel • 5 oz Ricotta • 3 tablespoons flour • 5 tablespoons apricot jam • 2 tablespoons rum • 3½ tablespoons fine plain chocolate

PREPARATION: Chop the walnut kernels and roast them. Beat the butter with ½ cup of sugar until it foams. Add yolk, lemon peel, Ricotta, flour and nuts. Froth the egg whites, add the remaining sugar and stir. Then put the mass in a greased cake pan with a diameter 9 in. Bake in a preheated oven at 392°F for about 30 minutes. The cake must rise and become firm. Leave the cake to cool in the pan and then remove it. Slightly mix the heated jam with the rum and spread this mixture over the cake. Sprinkle with flakes of grated chocolate.

IN THE KITCHEN

AROMA:
Ricotta is slightly sweet with a fine, acidulous, milky flavor.

FAT CONTENT:
20% fat in dry mass.

USE:
Ricotta has multiple uses. It is served with bread and sweet ingredients such as jam or fruit, but also with savory herbs or shrimps. With several leaves of rucola, it makes a good antipasto. In Italy, Ricotta is used for filling canneloni or crèpes along with with spinach or other vegetables, and in the preparation of cakes and pastry.

PURCHASE/STORAGE:
Ricotta can be obtained in specialized cheese shops or in Italian specialty shops. It cannot be kept for long time unless it is well-packed in foil in the refrigerator.

HAVE YOU TRIED…?

COFFEE-RICOTTA-CREAM: Mix Ricotta with sugar, espresso and a little rum to a smooth mixture. Pour into cups and set overnight in a cool place. Serve decorated with coffee beans.

Rocamadour

Milk:

Country of origin:
France

Recommended
drink:
White wine from
Bergerac
or red wine from
Cahors

■ TYPE: soft cheese

■ ORIGIN AND EXTENT: Rocamadour comes from the department of Lot in the Midi-Pyrenées region of southwest France.

■ FEATURES: Rocamadour has diameter of 2 in und the height less than 1 in. Its ivory-colored curd is soft and becomes firmer with maturity. The cheese is surrounded by a fine natural rind. After a longer maturation period, a light covering of blue mold may appear on the surface.

■ PRODUCTION: During the production of Rocamadour, only raw goat's milk from Alpine or Saan goats can be used. The farmer must not raise more than 10 animals per hectare of land. The goats must be fed at least 80% wheat, corn, oats and barley. The milk is soured by natural rennet immediately after the milking takes place and then the curd is filled to small molds. After formation and salting, the cheeses are stored in cellars at constant temperatures and prescribed air humidity.

IN THE KITCHEN

AROMA:

Rocamadour has a fine hazelnut flavor which becomes more intense as the cheese matures. It has an unobtrusive goat smell.

FAT CONTENT:

45% fat in dry mass.

USE:

Rocamadour is traditionally served at the end of the meal.

PURCHASE/STORAGE:

Rocamadour can be found in specialized cheese shops. Store it whole for a short time, well-packed, in the vegetable box of a refrigerator.

DID YOU KNOW THAT...?

Formerly this cheese was called Cabécou de Rocamadour. When translated from the Provencal dialect, it means "small goat cheese." Already in the 15th century, this cheese was a means of paying taxes and farm rent. In 1451, an agreement between feudal lord, the bishop of Evreux, and his vassals stated that taxes must be paid by the delivery of Rocamadour cheese.

Roncal

Milk:
🐑 🥛

Country of origin:
Spain

Recommended
drink:
Heavy red wine,
e.g. Rioja or
Navarra

■ TYPE: hard cheese

■ ORIGIN AND EXTENT: The cheese originates from seven villages in the valley of Roncal in the northern part of the Navarre region.

■ FEATURES: Roncal has a cylindrical shape with a brown or straw-colored rind. Its weight is between 3 and 7 lbs depending on size. The cheese is whitish-yellow and firm with only a few holes.

■ PRODUCTION: Roncal is produced exclusively from the milk of Latxa and Navarre sheep and a cross breed of Latxa. The cheese is made according to an old manual procedure. The souring is done with natural rennet or by the addition of fermented milk. Roncal matures at least 5 months.

■ HISTORICAL NOTE: Since the forest and meadows were utilized by the villages, the shepherds passed through the valley of Roncal. The sheep spent the winter in the southern part of Navarre and in the summer, they enjoyed the pasture in the valley. The production of cheese was important for the economy of the region.

IN THE KITCHEN

AROMA:
Roncal flavor is piquant, but the sheep aroma develops fully only with age.

FAT CONTENT:
50% fat in dry mass.

USE:
Young Roncal is eaten with bread. It is also well suited for baking in vegetable and meat dishes.

PURCHASE/STORAGE:
Roncal can be found in cheese shops or in Spanish specialty shops. It can be stored, well-packed, in the vegetable box of a refrigerator.

Roquefort

Milk:
🐑 ▯

Country of origin:
France

Recommended
drink:
Red wine, e.g.
Châteauneuf -
du - Pape,
or sweet wine,
e.g. Sauternes

■ TYPE: Semi-hard, sliced cheese with internal mold

■ ORIGIN AND EXTENT: The home of Roquefort is the former province of Rouergue. The traditional area for milk collection is situated in the Aveyron department and in the border departments of Aude, Gard, Hérlaut, Lozère and Tarn. Today, the sheep's milk can also be imported from Corsica and Pyrenees to satisfy the demands for cheese. But Roquefort must mature in the caves of Roquefort-sur-Soulzon in the Midi-Pyrénées region.

■ FEATURES: Roquefort is a cylindrical cheese with the diameter of 7½ to 8 in and a height of 4 to 39 in. Its weight ranges from 5½ to 7 lbs. The cheese has practically no rind and its soft, crumbly, cream-colored curds are striped with veins of green gray mold. Aluminum foil keeps the cheese from drying up.

■ PRODUCTION: The raw sheep's milk is heated and soured by the addition of rennet. Inoculation with penicillin is performed simultaneously. While the whey is dripping, the cheese is turned over five times per day. After salting, the cheeses are transported to Roquefort to mature for at least 3 months in the mountain of Combalou. The air penetrates

through long fissures in the rock, known as "Fleurines," into the hollow in the mountain. Roquefort can, therefore, mature in unique, but natural climatic conditions.

▬ HISTORICAL NOTE: Charlemagne proclaimed Roquefort his favorite cheese. In April 1411, Charles VI signed a Charter giving the inhabitants of Roquefort the exclusive right to perform the maturation of this cheese.

Apple – onion Quiche

▬ INGREDIENTS: 5 oz Roquefort • 1 cup flour • salt • 5 tablespoons margarine • 1 onion • ½ to 1 lb apples • 3 tablespoons butter • 3 eggs • 5 oz double cream • Provencal herbs • 1/2 bunch of parsley • pepper

▬ PREPARATION: Put the flour in the dish with a pinch of salt, add margarine and 3 oz crumbled cheese, mix with 2 tablespoons water and knead until the dough is smooth. Place in a cool place. Finely chop the onion. Peel and quarter the apples, remove the cores and grate finely. Melt 5 tablespoonsbutter in pan and stew with the onion until the onion bits are glassy. Add the apple mass and stew together, then cool.

Roll out the dough, put it into a greased dish and leave it again in a cool place. Then bake the dough in the oven at 374°F for 10 minutes until golden.

Wash the parsley and chop it finely. Beat together the eggs, double cream, herbs, parsley, salad and pepper. Insert 2 oz cheese into the egg mixture. Put the mixture of apples and onion onto the dough, pour the egg mixture over it and spread the remaining cheese over all. Bake in the oven at 374°F for 20 minutes until golden.

IN THE KITCHEN

AROMA:

Roquefort has a piquant, salty flavor slightly reminiscent of sheep and faintly of mold.

FAT CONTENT:

52% fat in dry mass.

USE:

Roquefort is essential for any cheese plate. It is also perfect for enhancing the flavor of sauces, preparing canapés, in salads, in soufflé, or as the filling of savory pastries. As a dessert, it is nice with fresh pears.

PURCHASE/STORAGE:

Roquefort can be found in cheese shops and also at cheese stands in larger supermarkets. This cheese is available throughout the year. It can be kept well-packed for several days in the vegetable box of a refrigerator.

HAVE YOU TRIED...?

PEARS WITH ROQUEFORT: **Halve 2 pears, remove the cores. Use a teaspoon to remove a little of the flesh from inside. Drip lemon juice in hollows. Mix the pear flesh with 2 tablespoons cream and 1½ oz. of crumbled Roquefort. Fill the pears with the mixture and spread with chopped walnuts.**

Sainte-Maure de Touraine

Milk:

Country of origin:
France

Recommended
drink:
Light, fruity red
and white wines
of Loire

▬ TYPE: soft cheese

▬ ORIGIN AND EXTENT: The home of Sainte-Maure de
Touraine is in the former province of Touraine on the Loire.
Today it is in the department Indre-et-Loire and the neighbor-
ing cantons of Loir-et-Cher, Indre and several near villages of
department of Vienne.

▬ FEATURES: The straw which passes through the center of
the Sainte-Maure de Touraine cheese enables one to distinguish it
quickly from other cheeses. The cheese is shaped like a roll with
a diameter of 2 to 3 in and a length of 11 in. The rind is covered by
light noble mold, but the cheese mostly has a jacket of ash. The
cheese is white and has a pasty consistency.

▬ PRODUCTION: Sainte-Maure de Touraine is produced
by adding a little rennet to goat's milk. The souring is performed in 24 hours. The curd is then poured into oblong
molds and may break slightly. The cheese is formed, slightly
salted and eventually spread with plant ash. The maturation
lasts at least 10 days.

▬ HISTORICAL NOTE: Raising goats and making cheese
have been traditional occupations in Sainte-Maure dating back

to Carolingian times. Sainte-Maure cheese is even cited in literature. The book "Touraine in time of Balzac" by M. Laurencin describes Sainte-Maure cheese.

▬ RELATED CHEESES: *Sainte-Maure* is a goat cheese from Touraine, but only Sainte-Maure de Touraine bears the AOC-impression.

Bechette d'Anjou. Bechette d'Anjou is similar to Sainte-Maure because it is oblong, rounded and also covered with ash. It has a mild flavor. The term for all these goat cheeses is "Chèvre."

Rolls of goat cheese are becoming more and more popular. They are mostly mild flavored with a weak fragrance characteristic of goat cheese. They are not only produced in France, but also in the Netherlands and Germany. In fact, they contain only a small portion of goat's milk and are mainly composed of cow's milk. The cheese gourmands tend to scorn these cheeses.

Fried goat cheese with green onion

■ INGREDIENTS: 9 oz Sainte-Maure de Touraine • 5 tablespoons breadcrumbs • 4 tablespoons olive oil • 2 bunches green onion with tops • 1 pinch mace • salt • black pepper

■ PREPARATION: Cut the goat cheese in slices and spread with breadcrumbs. Fry the cheese slices in a pan in olive oil. Pare the onions, slice them in two longitudinally and cut them up into 1 in pieces. Heat the onions briefly in the oil, and add spices. Serve the cheese and onions together.

IN THE KITCHEN

AROMA:
Sainte-Maure de Touraine has a mild mushroom flavor with a characteristic goat aroma, which is stronger when the cheese is older.

FAT CONTENT:
45% fat in dry mass.

USE:
Sainte-Maure de Touraine can cut into slices as canapés to accompany an aperitif. The cheese is also suitable for gratination and may be served with salad or fruit.

PURCHASE/STORAGE:
Sainte-Maure de Touraine and variations can be found in specialized cheese shops. The best time to buy this goat cheese is at the beginning of March and in November. The cheese can be kept, well-packed, for several days in the vegetable box of a refrigerator.

Saint-Nectaire

Milk:
🐄 🥛

Country of origin:
France

Recommended drink:
Light, fruity red wine,
e.g. Beaujolais

TYPE: Semi-hard, sliced cheese

ORIGIN AND EXTENT: For centuries, Sainte-Nectaire was produced in the Monts-Dore region in Auvergne. Today, it is also produced in the northern part of the department of Cantal and in the southwest part of the Puy-de-Dôme department.

FEATURES: Saint-Nectaire has a fine mold rind ranging in color from whitish yellow to red. The cheese is supple and elastic and responds to light pressure exerted by the thumb. The cheese comes in two sizes: the first with a weight of 4½ lb, a diameter of 8 in and a height of 2 in and the other with a weight of only 1 lb, a diameter of 5 in and a height of 1½ in. The smaller variant is called Petit Saint-Nectaire. When it is produced by hand, it has a green elliptical stamp whereas industrially produced cheese has a rectangular stamp.

PRODUCTION: The milk is heated to 90°F and soured by the rennet. The curd is subsequently broken and pressed into molds. After salting, the cheese is folded in a cloth and undergoes a new pressing. During the 21 day period of maturation, the cheese is regularly washed with salty water, thus stimulating the development of white, yellow or red flora on its

surface. Handmade Saint-Nectaire is produced using the morning and evening milk immediately after milking. It matures for 6 weeks on rye straw in natural cellars dug in the volcanic rock.

■ HISTORICAL NOTE: The French field marshal, Henri de La Ferté-Senneterre, brought Saint-Nectaire cheese to the court of Louis XIV. The popularity of the cheese with the French nobility made him famous.

Baked Toast

▬ INGREDIENTS: 2 small onions • 1 garlic clove • 1 table-spoon olive oil • 1½ to 3 oz tomato pulp • Provencal herbs • 2 big tomatoes • 1 can of sardines • 6 slices toasted bread • salt and pepper • 1 cup capers • 6 thick slices of Saint Nectaire (about 9 oz)

▬ PREPARATION: Cut the onions and garlic into small cubes and stew them in oil. Add the tomato pulp and herbs. Boil briefly. Cut the tomatoes to thin slices, let the sardines drain and mince. Slightly roast the toast and grease with the tomato pulp mixture. Dress the toasts with tomato slices and flavor with salt and pepper. Then add the sardines, capers and cheese slices. Bake in a preheated oven at of 392°F until the cheese is melted.

IN THE KITCHEN

AROMA:
Saint-Nectaire has an agreeably full, nutty and slightly spicy flavor. It smells faintly of cellar potatoes.

FAT CONTENT:
45% fat in dry mass.

USE:
Saint-Nectaire is consumed after a meal and is an ingredient in many regional dishes. It is also used to flavor soups and for baking.

PURCHASE/STORAGE:
Saint-Nectaire can be found in cheese shops. A whole piece can be kept for several days wrapped in grease-proof paper and sealed in a plastic container in the vegetable box of the refrigerator.

HAVE YOU TRIED...?
SAINT-NECTAIRE ON PEARS WITH GRAPE SAUCE: **Peel the pears and cut into slices, add slices of cheese and gratinate them in the oven. Remove seeds from grapes, mince them to a purée, mix with a little warm honey, oil and vinegar and add pepper and salt according to taste. Pour this sauce on a plate and place the pears with the cheese in the sauce. Bon appetit!**

Salers

Milk:
🐄 🥛

Country of origin:
France

Recommended
drink:
Red wine,
e.g. Beaujolais

■ TYPE: Sliced cheese

■ ORIGIN AND EXTENT: Salers comes from Auvergne. Today, it is produced in the department of Cantal as well as in 41 villages in the Aveyron, Corrèze, Haute-Loire and Puy de Dôme departments.

■ FEATURES: Salers has a cylindrical shape and can be easily recognized by its red aluminum label. It has a thick, naturally dry rind on which molds grow easily. It comes in various sizes with a diameter ranging from 15 to 16 in and a weight between 77 and 121 lb.

■ PRODUCTION: Salers is produced only between 1 May and 31 October. The cow's milk is immediately soured by rennet after milking and subsequently minced and pressed. Then the curd is minced again, salted, molded and pressed for 48 hours in a cheese press. It matures in wet cellars for at least 1 month, or up to 1 year.

IN THE KITCHEN

AROMA:

Salers has a slightly acidulous and mildly spicy flavor. It smells faintly of fruit.

FAT CONTENT:

45% fat in dry mass.

USE:

Salers is usually consumed after the meal. It complements apples, grapes and red fruit well. It is also used for baking and for flavoring soups and sauces.

PURCHASE/STORAGE:

Salers can be found in specialized cheese shops. It can be kept whole, packed in grease-proof paper and perforated aluminum foil, in the vegetable box of a refrigerator.

DID YOU KNOW THAT...?

Salers is closely related to Cantal and therefore has a similar history and origin. The name comes from the town of Salers located in the heart of the Cantal mountains at a height of slightly more than half a mile.

Samsö

Milk:
🐄 🥛

Country of origin:
Denmark

Recommended
drink:
Red wine, e.g.
late Burgundy

■ TYPE: Sliced cheese

■ ORIGIN AND EXTENT: Samsö is a product of Swiss cheese-makers who developed this cheese in the 19th century from Danish cows' milk for the kingdom of Denmark. The cheese is named after an island in the Baltic between Fünen and Seeland.

■ FEATURES: Samsö is a flat, round, or sometimes block-shaped cheese. The cheese is straw-colored and has a few hazelnut sized holes. Its thin, yellow rind is often covered with a layer of wax.

■ PRODUCTION: Samsö is made from pasteurized cow's milk. The milk is soured by rennet, minced and heated again while stirred. Then the cheese is formed, pressed and salted. Samsö matures for at least 3 months.

In the kitchen

Aroma:
Samsö has a mild and nutty flavor. The flavor remains mild even after a longer maturation period.

Fat content:
45% fat in dry mass.

Use:
Samsö is eaten with bread as well as in hot dishes. It melts easily and is therefore suitable for soufflés, toasts or fried eggs.

Purchase/storage:
Samsö can be found in specialized cheese shops. It should be kept whole, packed in greaseproof paper and perforated aluminum foil, in the vegetable box of a refrigerator.

São Jorge

Milk:
🐄 🥛

Country of origin:
Portugal

Recommended drink:
Young white wine,
e.g. Vinho verde

■ TYPE: Hard cheese

■ ORIGIN AND EXTENT: The cheese comes from the island of São Jorge in the Azores.

■ FEATURES: Jorge is a large, round shaped cheese with a diameter of 8 to 14 in and a height of 4 to 6 in. Its weight ranges between 18 to 26 lbs. The consistency of the cheese is firm and shows several holes. The rind is hard and dark yellow colored a may be covered by a layer of paraffin.

■ PRODUCTION: São Jorge is produced from raw cow's milk. After souring, the whey is left to drain slowly. Then the cheese is put into molds, pressed and matured for at least three months.

■ HISTORICAL NOTE: The instructions for the preparation of this cheese probably came from English sailors, marooned on the island. The preparation procedure is similar to that of the English cheese, Cheddar.

IN THE KITCHEN

AROMA:
São Jorge has a light and salty flavor and a spicy aroma.

FAT CONTENT:
45% fat in dry mass.

USE:
São Jorge cut in small cubes is offered with wine or can be grated to enhance baked dishes or soups and sauces.

PURCHASE/STORAGE:
São Jorge can be found in specialized cheese shops or in shops which stock Portuguese specialties. It can be kept whole, well-packed, in the vegetable box of a refrigerator.

Sbrinz

Milk:
🐄 ◻

Country of origin:
Switzerland

Recommended
drink: Red wine,
e.g. late
Burgundy

■ TYPE: Hard cheese

■ ORIGIN AND EXTENT: Sbrinz is produced in 42 selected cheese factories in the valleys and mountains of Switzerland. Sbrinz is produced exclusively from the milk of the region and is also stored in the cellars of local dairies.

■ FEATURES: The weight of this round cheese ranges between 44 and 99 lbs. Its diameter is 20 to 28 in and its height is about 5½ in. The rind is golden-yellow or brown, firm and dry. The pale yellow or ivory cheese is crumbly and dry.

■ PRODUCTION: The milk comes from cows fed on hay and grass, but never on silage. For the production of the cheese, the milk is heated while stirred and then soured by rennet. The curd is cut into uniform pieces with a wire knife and the whey is separated from the cheese mass. The cheese is then poured into molds and pressed until the whey has finished draining. The cheeses are placed in a salt bath for 18 days and stored for 2 months at 64°F. During the maturation period, the cheese loses fat and much water. Then it is turned over and stored for another 22 months to make it extra hard.

■■■ HISTORICAL NOTE: Sbrinz is among the oldest Swiss cheeses. It was produced in the time of the Romans and was known as "caseus helveticus" and highly valued for its durability. Sbrinz was transported to Rome and served as provisions for the legionaries during their field expeditions.

Gnocchi (dumplings) with sage and tomatoes

INGREDIENTS: 3 lbs potatoes, boiled to floury consistency • 3 lb tomatoes • 2 shallots • 2 tablespoons sunflower oil • salt and pepper • 3 egg whites • 1 cup flour • 1 tablespoon butter • 12 leaves of sage • 2½ oz Sbrinz

PREPARATION: Peel and quarter tomatoes, remove the core and cut into small cubes and finely chop the shallots.
Heat oil in the pan, stew the shallots until translucent. Add the

tomato chunks and flavor with salt and pepper. Let mixture simmer for ten minutes.
Peel the still-hot potatoes, force them through a potato press, mix with yolk, salt and flour and knead to make the dough supple. Using a teaspoon, make small gnocchi, flatten them with a fork and place in boiling water. After boiling, remove them with a ladle. Melt the butter and fry the sage leaves. Remove the leaves from the butter and pour the butter on the gnocchi. Distribute the gnocchi on plates, dress with tomato sauce and sage leaves, and sprinkle on grated Sbrinz cheese.

In the kitchen

Aroma:
The flavor of the cheese is aromatically spicy and piquant.

Fat content:
45% fat in dry mass.

Use:
The cheese is very well suited to grating, shaving and melting and is therefore ideal for baking into dishes or for flavoring soups and sauces.

Purchase/storage:
Sbrinz can only be found in specialized cheese shops. It should be kept whole, wrapped in grease-proof paper and perforated aluminum foil, in the refrigerator.

Schabziger

Milk:

🐄 🥛

Country of origin:
Switzerland

Recommended
drink:
White wine,
e.g. Fendant

━━ TYPE: Hard cheese

━━ ORIGIN AND EXTENT: Schabziger is an old monastery cheese from the canton of Glarus. It is still prepared in the Glarus Alps.

━━ FEATURES: Schabziger is striking due to its small conical cylinder shape, green color and light weight of only 7 oz. The cheese has no rind and is remarkably firm.

━━ PRODUCTION: Skimmed milk is used in the production of Schabziger. The milk is heated in a kettle and soured by lactic acid bacteria. The milk protein is coagulated and the curd is separated from the whey. The cheese matures for 4 to 12 weeks and is known as Rohziger. After this phase of maturation, the Rohziger is grated and mixed with salt. The cheese is subsequently stored for additional maturing for about 3 months in silos and is weighted down. The cheese obtains its distinctive green color when mixed with minced clover. It is then pressed into a mold in the shape of a conical cylinder.

━━ HISTORICAL NOTE: The first written mention of Schabzigers is from the 8th century. Until 1395, the Glarus land belonged to the monastery of Säckingen and the inhabi-

tants paid rent to the monks. Rent could be paid in cheese. But the local cheese tasted dull and therefore its flavor was improved with the aromatic Bockshorn clover, brought from the Orient by knights during the Crusades.

Choux pastry cheese wreath

INGREDIENTS: 1 cup water • 5 tablespoons butter • ½ cup flour • 3 eggs • 5 oz Greyerzer or Emmentaler • salt and pepper • 3½ oz Schabziger • 2 bunches of chives • 5 oz cream • 5 oz curd cheese • 9 oz Quark

PREPARATION: Boil the water, butter and salt together. Add the flour to the boiling water. Stir thoroughly with a ladle until the bottom clouds, then remove the pot from the fire and add the yolks while beating vigorously. Form a wreath with the mixture on a greased baking sheet. Bake in the oven preheated to 392°F. Allow the wreath to cool the Schabziger mixture.

Prepare the filling from grated Schabziger, chopped chives and whipped cream. Mix the cream cheese with the Quark, add and then cut horizontally in half and mix well. Fill the wreath with the filling.

IN THE KITCHEN

AROMA:
The flavor of Schabziger is aromatic and spicy, but the clover distinguishes it from other cheeses.

FAT CONTENT:
1% absolute fat.

USE:
Schabziger is a grating cheese. It is usually added to soups, sauces, noodle and potato dishes, or it can be spread over these dishes.

PURCHASE/STORAGE:
Schabziger can only be found in specialized cheese shops. It must be kept whole, wrapped in grease-proof paper and perforated aluminum foil, in the refrigerator.

Selles-sur-Cher

Milk:

Country of origin:
France

Recommended
drink:
Light fruity red
wine,
e.g. Chinon

■ TYPE: soft cheese

■ ORIGIN AND EXTENT: Selles-sur-Cher is principally produced in the village of the same name on the Loire River. As bearer of the AOC–impression, it may be produced only in the departments of Loire-et-Cher, Indre and Cher.

■ FEATURES: Selles-sur-Cher is a round, soft cheese with a diameter of 3½ in, a height of 1 in and a weight of about 5 oz. Its surface is covered with ash and a layer of blue and white mold. The white curd has a very firm consistency. The cheese is sold without packaging.

■ PRODUCTION: Selles-sur-Cher is produced from goat's milk soured with a small amount of rennet. The curd is poured into molds from which the whey is drained. The molds are lined with salt and plant ash so that the cheeses do not stick. The period of maturation ranges from 10 days to 3 weeks.

IN THE KITCHEN

AROMA:

The flavor of Selles-sur-Cher is mild and nutty, but becomes more pungent with age. It smells faintly of goats.

FAT CONTENT:

45% fat in dry mass.

USE:

Selles-sur-Cher is a typical dessert cheese which is served at the end of a meal. Connoisseurs do not remove the rind because it has a lovely aroma.

PURCHASE/STORAGE:

Selles-sur-Cher and its variants can be found in specialized cheese shops. The best time for goat cheese begins in early summer and ends in fall. It must be kept, well-packed, in the vegetable box of a refrigerator.

RELATED SORTS

Coeur de Selles **is the same cheese, but heart-shaped.**

Pavé blésois **is a rectangular variant from Blois au Loire.**

Pavé Touraine **is also rectangular. "Pavé" means "paving stone."**

Serra da Estrela

Milk:

Country of origin:
Portugal

Recommended
drink:
Red wine,
e.g. Redondo

■ TYPE: Semi-hard, sliced cheese

■ ORIGIN AND EXTENT: Farmers and goat shepherds traditionally prepared Serra da Estrella in the mountainous region of Serra da Estrela in central Portugal. Today, the cheese is also produced in the regions of Mangualde, Celorico da Beira, Tondela, Gouveia, Penalva, Fornos de Algordes and Carregal do Sal.

■ FEATURES: Serra da Estrela is a small, round mountain cheese with diameter of 6 to 7 in and a height of 2 to 2½ in. The weight ranges between 3 and 4 lbs. The pale yellow cheese is soft and creamy and has no holes. The rind is firm and hard. Fissures occur on the surface.

■ PRODUCTION: Serra da Estrela is produced from raw sheep's milk. The milk is soured by the sap of the thistle *Cynara cardunculus*. The whey is left to drain slowly. After salting, the cheese matures for at least 30 days, a period divided into two phases. Serra da Estrela is first stored in wet rooms and later in cool, dry cellars or caves.

IN THE KITCHEN

AROMA:
Serra da Estrela is mildly spicy.

FAT CONTENT:
45% fat in dry mass.

USE:
Serra da Estrela complements an aperitif well, harmonizing nicely with other cheeses on a cheese plate.

PURCHASE/STORAGE:
Serra da Estrela can be found in specialized cheese shops or in shops carrying Portuguese specialties. It must be kept whole, well-packed, in the vegetable box of a refrigerator.

DID YOU KNOW THAT...?
Traditionally, this cheese is produced during the winter months from November to March. It can, of course, mature longer than 30 days, which will make it harder and more strongly flavored.

Stilton

Milk:
🐄 🥛

Country of origin:
Great Britain

Recommended
drink:
Dessert wine,
e.g. Port

TYPE: Sliced cheese with blue mold

COUNTRY OF ORIGIN: The noblest cheese in England comes from the counties of Derbyshire, Leicestershire and Nottinghamshire in central England.

FEATURES: Stilton has the shape of a high cylinder and a weight of about 18 lbs. The rind is thick, wrinkled and firm, its color is brown-gray with white spots of mold. A young Stilton is ivory colored, resembling marble, and has a crumbly consistency. Older cheese is creamier, darker and more prominently veined with blue mold.

PRODUCTION: Stilton is produced from pasteurized cow's milk. The curd is cut up with a wire knife and mold culture is added. After 24 hours of dripping in dripping tanks, the curd is cut again and salted. It is then put into molds and left to sit about 1 week while being regularly turned over. Then the cheese is removed from the molds and matured for about 12 weeks. In this phase, the cheese must be pierced two to three times to enable the penetration of air, thus enabling the development of the culture.

■■■ HISTORICAL NOTE: Stilton was first popularized at Bell Inn, a resting place for travelers from London to York. The guests consumed – and greatly enjoyed – bread and cheese veined with blue mold. This cheese became known all over the world as Stilton.

Beef fillet with Stilton cream

■ INGREDIENTS: 4 beef fillets • 4 slices white bread • 3½ oz Stilton • 3 tablespoons butter • 2 tablespoons cream • 1 tablespoon parsley • 20 shallots • slightly less than ½ cup red wine • 3–4 tablespoons of bouillon • salt and pepper

■ PREPARATION: Toast the slices of bread and cut to fit the size of the fillets. Melt 2 tablespoons butter in the pan and stew chopped shallots until soft. Remove shallots from pan and put aside in a warm place. In the same pan, boil red wine, add bouillon, boil again and season to taste.

Mix the stilton, butter, cream and parsley, with salt and pepper to taste.

Pan-fry the meat on both sides, put them on the slices of toast with a little stilton cream. Arrange the shallots around the fillets and pour a little red wine sauce over them.

IN THE KITCHEN

AROMA:
Stilton has a spicy flavor with becomes sharper with age.

FAT CONTENT:
52% fat in dry mass.

USE:
Stilton is traditionally consumed in England as a dessert cheese. But it is also delicious on bread and good in salads or as a filling for baked potatoes.

HAVE YOU TRIED ...?

In England, Stilton is offered at the end of a meal with a glass of Port. Stilton should be taken out of the refrigerator several hours before consumption. Wrap it in foil to keep in its aroma.

PURCHASE/STORAGE:
Stilton can be found in cheese shops. Well-wrapped in grease-proof paper and in a plastic box, it can be stored in the vegetable compartment of a refrigerator.

Svecia

Milk:

🐄 🥛

Country of origin:
Sweden

Recommended
drink:
Beer, e.g. Pilsen
In kitchen

TYPE: Sliced cheese

ORIGIN AND EXTENT: Svecia is a Swedish copy of Dutch Gouda and Edamer. Thanks to the union of Hanse, Dutch cheeses appeared in Sweden and the Swedes tried to make a similar cheese. The result of this is Svecia.

FEATURES: Svecia has the shape of a cartwheel, and a diameter of 12 in and a height of 5 in. The weight is about 44 lb. The cheese has a firm consistency and contains a few small holes. The rind is covered by wax.

PRODUCTION: Svecia is produced from pasteurized cow's milk. The milk is soured by rennet, cut up, poured into molds and pressed. After salting, the cheese matures for at least three months and then can be sold. The more mature variant matures up to 1 year and its aroma is spicier. Svecia is also produced with cloves and caraway seeds. Svecia cheeses can be recognized by a distinctive red wax coating.

In the kitchen

Aroma:
The flavor of young Svecia is fine and mild and that of the mature cheese is stronger and more piquant.

Fat content:
28% fat in dry mass.

Use:
In Sweden, Svecia is consumed mainly with bread. Variants with higher fat content can also be used for baking.

Purchase/storage:
Svecia can be found in specialized cheese shops. It can be stored as a whole piece wrapped in grease-proof paper and aluminum foil in the vegetable box of a refrigerator.

Have you tried ...?
Swedes enjoy Svecia with bread or toast .

Taleggio

Milk:
🐄 🥛

Country of origin:
Italy

Recommended drink:
Red wine,
e.g. Barbaresco

■ TYPE: Semi-hard, sliced cheese

■ ORIGIN AND EXTENT: Taleggio is an Italian cheese produced in the provinces of Bergamo, Brescia, Como, Cremona, Mailand, Pavia, Treviso and Novara.

■ FEATURES: Taleggio is a flat, square cheese. Each edge measures about 8 in. The weight ranges from 4 to 5 lbs. The rind is thin and reddish. The soft curd is white to straw yellow.

■ PRODUCTION: Taleggio is produced from raw cow's milk. The cheese is salted and dried. The maturation lasts for 40 days at a temperature of 37° to 46°F with high humidity.

■ HISTORICAL NOTE: Taleggio is one of the oldest cheeses in Lombardy. It has been known since the 9th century. Formerly, it was produced in the valley of the same name, where the cows pasture at heights of 6,000 feet.

■ RELATED CHEESES: *Quercino* has the pale green spots of rare noble mold, but its fat content is 55%.

IN THE KITCHEN

AROMA:
The flavor of Taleggio is spicy, nutty and fresh. Its smell is slightly reminiscent of a cow.

FAT CONTENT:
48% fat in dry mass.

USE:
Taleggio served with fruits and walnuts is the ideal finishing touch to an Italian meal. As a snack with tomatoes or with Radicchio salad, the cheese is especially favored in Lombardy. Its good melting qualities make it perfect for risotto or polenta.

PURCHASE/STORAGE:
Taleggio can be found in a cheese shop or in an Italian delicatessen. Well-packed, it can be kept in the vegetable box of a refrigerator for several days.

Tête de Moine

Milk:
🐄 🥛

*Country
of origin:
Switzerland*

*Recommended
drink:
Red or white
wine, e.g. late
Burgundy or
Fendant*

▬ TYPE: Hard cheese

▬ ORIGIN AND EXTENT: This cheese has its origin in the monastery of Bellelay. Today, this geographically protected cheese is produced in Prunt, Moutier and Courtelary Saulcy as well as in many cheese factories in Courgenay in Jura.

▬ FEATURES: Tête de Moine is striking due to its small diameter and relatively large height. The cylindrical cheese has a diameter of 4 to 6 in. The height is 28 in and the weight ranges between ½ to 4½ lb. The rind is firm, greasy, grainy and wet and red-brown colored.

▬ PRODUCTION: The milk comes from cows, which are fed hay and grass, but never silage. The milk must be processed for 24 hours after milking. The raw milk is heated in copper kettles at temperature not exceeding 100°F before it is soured by rennet. The curd is cut up by means of a wire knife, heated again and then pressed. The cheeses lie at least 12 hours in a salty bath. During the maturation, the cheese is regularly treated with salty water to stimulate the formation of grease on the rind. Then the cheese matures at least 6 months on spruce boards.

In the kitchen

AROMA:
The flavor of Tête de Moine is mildly spicy.

FAT CONTENT:
51% fat in dry mass.

USE:
Tête de Moine is not sliced, but scraped. For this purpose, it is best to use the girolla, a special tool for scraping this cheese. The upper layer of the cheese is removed and the girolla is put on the center of the cheese. By rotating the cheese clockwise, it is scraped. The shape of the scraped mass of cheese resembles the shaven head of a monk and for this it has been called "monk's head."

PURCHASE/STORAGE:
Tête de Moine can be obtained in specialized cheese shops. At home, it is best to store it whole in the refrigerator, wrapped in grease-proof paper and perforated foil.

DID YOU KNOW THAT...?

Tête de Moine was mentioned as early as 1192 as the cheese of the monastery of Bellelay. Old documents give evidence that this cheese served as a means of payment. During the French Revolution in 1797, the monks were expelled from the monastery, but the cheese was still produced in the old monastery cheese workshops.

Tetilla

Milk:
🐄 🥛

Country of origin:
Spain

Recommended drink:
Red wine, e.g. Rioja

▬ TYPE: Semi-hard, sliced cheese

▬ ORIGIN AND EXTENT: The home of Tetilla is Galicia. The small villages and scattered yards, mildly undulating country and cold sea climate of Galicia, in northwest Spain, make the area ideal for cattle-raising.

▬ FEATURES: Tetilla is characterized by its conical shape. The cheese is soft and creamy with a rather indistinct rind.

▬ PRODUCTION: Tetilla is produced from pasteurized cow's milk from Rubia Gallega and Frisona cows. The milk is soured using industrially produced or natural rennet at about 86°F. The curd is then pressed and salted. The time of maturation is 1 week to several months.

In the kitchen

Aroma:
Tetilla has a slightly sharp, buttery flavor. Its mild aroma makes it popular with children.

Fat content:
45% fat in dry mass.

Use:
Thanks to its good melting qualities, Tetilla is suitable for baking or can be crumbed and fried. Traditionally Tetilla is consumed with quince jam, bread and wine.

Purchase/storage:
Tetilla can be found in specialized cheese shops or in a shop carrying Spanish specialties. It must be stored, well-packed, in the vegetable box of a refrigerator.

Tilsiter

■ TYPE: Semi-hard, sliced cheese

■ ORIGIN AND EXTENT: The home of Tilsiter is on the river Memel in the town of Tilsit. This cheese originated in the first half of the 19th century. Tilsiter cheese is one of the traditional cheeses of Northern Germany and is well-known, especially along the coast.

■ FEATURES: Tilsiter is now mostly offered as a block. Its ivory to yellow curd is greasy and shows many small holes. It usually lacks a rind, but formerly it had a rind of red grease which gave the cheese an extra strong aroma.

■ PRODUCTION: Tilsiter is usually produced from pasteurized cow's milk. In several farmhouses, it is produced from raw milk. After being cut up, the curd is poured into forms, but not pressed. Due to its own weight, the resulting cheese has many holes. Traditional Tilsiters are rubbed with red grease. The cheese matures at least 5 weeks. If it has a red culture, it is washed with this mold and salt solution several times during the maturation.

■ HISTORICAL NOTE: The first mention of Tilsiter comes from a Mrs. Westphal who lived in a farm house at Tilsit in

Eastern Prussia around 1840. But the recipe is probably much older. It is possible that the Dutch who migrated to Tilsit wanted to prepare Gouda and produced Tilsiter instead.

■■■ RELATED CHEESES: *Wilstermar cheese* is named after the fertile strip of earth at the river Elbe near Hamburg, where it was first produced. This cheese usually matures in four weeks even without the use of red grease. For sale, it is packed in foil and it is clearly finer than other variants.

Steinbusch cheese obtained its name from Steinbusch in Pomerania. It is a small cheese which matures in three weeks. Since cultures of red mold are introduced into the cheese, it has an extra spicy flavor.

Tollenser cheese may be produced only in the districts of Malchin, Altentreptow, Teterow, Demmin, Neubrandenburg and Stadt Neubrandenburg. The cheese is made in the same way as Tilsiter, but with red mold. The flavor of the cheese is very intense. It is best consumed during brunch with dark bread and a glass of beer or a shot of brandy.

In the kitchen

Aroma:

Tilsiter without red culture has a mild flavor. But when prepared traditionally, its flavor becomes spicy and intense. Its smell is strong.

Fat content:

30 to 60 % fat in dry mass.

Use:

Tilsiter is cut into slices and consumed with bread. Some pickles and beets suit the cheese well. Tilsiter cheese with a greater fat content is also suitable for baking.

Purchase/storage:

Tilsiter can be obtained wrapped in foil in any supermarket. Strong Tilsiter with red culture can be found only in specialized cheese shops. Tightly sealed in a box and kept in the refrigerator, it will remain edible for a few days.

Valençay

Milk:

Country of origin:
France

Recommended
drink:
White wine,
e.g. Chablis

■ TYPE: Soft cheese

■ ORIGIN AND EXTENT: The home of Valençay is in the southern part of the Loire Valley in the departments Loire-et-Cher, Indre-et-Loire and Cher.

■ FEATURES: Valençay is a small cheese and has the shape of a pyramid without a tip. This soft goat cheese has a fine, structured consistency and a naturally created rind. The surface is either natural or spread with ash. The weight is between 7 to 9 oz.

■ PRODUCTION: Valençay is produced from goat's milk soured by a very small amount of rennet. The curd is packed into molds and the whey drains. After the cheeses have been taken out of the molds, they are spread with a mixture of noble mold and plant ash. Then Valençay matures for two weeks in air with 80% humidity.

In the kitchen

Aroma:
Valençay has a moderate and fine, slightly nutty flavor.

Fat content:
45% fat in dry mass.

Use:
Valençay is a typical dessert cheese which completes a meal. Thanks to its moderate aroma and curious shape, it is a worthy addition to any cheese plate.

Purchase/storage:
Valençay can be found in specialized cheese shops. This cheese is available throughout the year. If well-packed, it can be stored for several days in the vegetable box of a refrigerator.

Did you know that...?

The legend of Valençay cheese says that this cheese used to be a perfect pyramid, but the shape was changed because of Napoleon. After his defeat in Egypt, Napoleon called at the castle of Valençay. The shape of the cheese reminded him of the Egyptian pyramids. Still smarting from his defeat, Napoleon slashed the tip of a pyramid off with his sword. Since that time, the cheese is a pyramid without a tip.

Weisslacker

Milk:
🐄 🥛

Country of origin:
Germany

Recommended drink:
Beer, e.g. white beer

■ TYPE: Semi-hard, sliced cheese

■ ORIGIN AND EXTENT: The cheese originates in Oberallgäu and is commonly called beer cheese. This cheese has a white grease on the surface, similar to lacquer.

■ FEATURES: Weisslacker does not have any rind. The texture is light and penetrated by a large numbers of holes. The cheeses weigh 2 to 4 lbs. The cheese is also packed in 2 oz blocks for self-service sale.

■ PRODUCTION: Weisslacker is produced from pasteurized cow's milk. After souring with rennet, it is cut up, ladled out of the whey and bathed for two days in a salty solution. The cheese is then transported to a cooled room to mature. It is regularly spread with salt and greased. For the last stage of maturation, it is wrapped in aluminum foil for 3 to 4 more months.

IN THE KITCHEN

AROMA:
The flavor of Weisslacker is strongly piquant, sharp and also salty.

FAT CONTENT:
45% fat in dry mass.

USE:
Weisslacker should be cut into bite-sized pieces and consumed with beer and pretzels. It can be also used for baking by mixing it into pastry or baking small squares of it with other ingredients.

PURCHASE/STORAGE:
Weisslacker can be found mostly in Bavaria, but outside Bavaria, it can only be found in specialized cheese shops. This cheese should be kept in refrigerator.

DID YOU KNOW THAT...?
Weisslacker was developed by the brothers Josef and Anton Kramer from Wertach in Allgäu. They developed this cheese in the year 1876 from "Backsteinkäse," the Limburger of Allgäu. By increasing the contents of dry substance, fat and salt, the durability was improved.

Index

Index of Cheese Recipes by Course

Information & Ideas Related to Cheese

Käserei-Museum/Museum of cheese-making
Rempartstraße 7
79346 Endingen
Tel.: 07642/68 99 90
Fax: 07642/68 99 99
E-Mail: info@endingen.de
Opening hours: Su 14 – 17 hours and according to agreement

Holländisches Käsemuseum/Het Hollands Kaasmuseum
Waagplein 2
(Waaggebouw)
1811 JP Alkmaar
Tel.: ++31/(0)72/511 42 84
Fax: ++31/(0)72/511 75 13
E-Mail: info@kaasmuseum.nl

Cheese market in Alkmaar
Each Friday morning (April to September) in national costumes on the market place
Cheese - bike trips
Six trips through Regions of Germany with special sorts of cheese.

You can order "Käsekarte" by sending a return envelop DIN A5 and 1,44 EUR stamp at: Information Office - Informationsbüro Deutscher Käse Nymphenburger Straße 86 80636 München Tel.: 089/124 451 25 Fax: 089/124 451 14 E-Mail: deutscher.kaese@ketchum.de

Exhibition cheese factory:
Käserei Obere Mühle
Hindelang – Bad Oberdorf
Tel.: 08324/28 57
Fax: 08324/86 35
E-Mail: info@obere-muehle.de
Internet: www.obere-muehle.de
Opening hours: from 10 to 13 hours and from 14 to 18 hours

Appenzeller cheese factory
CH – 9063 Stein
Tel.: ++41/71 368 50 70
Fax: ++41/71 368 50 75
E-Mail: info@schaukae-serei-stein.ch
Internet: www.show-cheese.ch

Cheese -Online-Shops:

Schreier
Maître Fromager
Schwarzwaldstraße 26
78224 Singen
Tel.: 07731/672 66
Fax.: 07731/697 42
E-Mail: salut@kaesereich-frankreich.de
Internet: www.kaesereich-frankreich.de

Käse Schuster
Im Rosental 1
61231 Nauheim
Tel.: 06032/920710
Fax: 06032/920711
E-Mail: info@kaese-schus-ter.de

Internet: www.kaese-schuster.de

All about Bio Cheese
Zurwies 11
88239 Wangen
Tel.: 07522/55 81
Fax.: 07522/809 39
E-Mail: shop@alles-biokaese.de
Internet: www.alles-biokaese.de

Chäs Marili
Beat Hofstetter
Fronwagplatz 9
CH – 8200 Schaffhausen
Tel.: ++41/(0)52/625 16 37
Fax: ++41/(0)52/625 18 63
E-Mail: info@chaes-mar-ili.ch
Internet: www.chaes-marili.ch

List of photographs

aid: S. 19, 20, 21, 22, 23, 25, 26, 27, 29, 36, 45, 47, 49, 81, 99, 103, 107, 111, 121, 125, 133, 161, 169, 193, 195, 211, 229, 231, 289, 290, 295

agrar-press: S. 13, 14, 16, 17, 18, 24,

APQE: S. 145

ArlaFoods bildbank und bsmart: S. 139, 281

Beck Käse vom Feinsten, München: S. 53, 57, 75, 113, 213, 239, 263, 283

Berglandmilch/unisono: S. 185

Consorzio Tutela Grana Padano: S. 129, 187, 196, 207

Cropwell Bishop Creamery: S. 277

denhay: S. 87

Galbani Deutschland GmbH: S. 183

Geska, Glarus: S. 269

Herve Société: S. 141

Het Nederlands Zuivelbureau: S. 159

Cheeses from Switzerland: S. 32 below, 101, 190, 235, 256, 265, 267, 285

Mejeriforeningen/Danish Dairy Board: S. 137, 261

Osttiroler Molkerei-genossenschaft: S. 131

Singleton's Dairy Ltd.: S. 91 oben

Sopexa: S. 39, 40, 43, 59, 63, 64, 67, 77, 78, 83, 85, 93, 95, 97, 105, 115, 153, 155, 163, 179, 189, 199, 203, 205, 217, 221, 223, 227, 237, 243, 247, 251, 255, 259, 273, 293

Spanish General Consulate: S. 73, 143, 147, 165, 171, 173, 175, 245, 287

Brigitte Sporrer/Alena Hrbkova: S. 50, 54, 60, 102, 110, 134, 156, 166, 180, 200, 208, 214, 224, 240, 248, 266, 270, 278

www.greece.org: S. 109

We thank WMF and Zwilling for the photographs on pages 30-32 All other photographs are from the archives of the Publishing House.